Joel Chandler Harris

Joel Chandler Harris

R. Bruce Bickley, Jr.

130186 ✓

Brown Thrasher Books

The University of Georgia Press

Athens and London

© 1978, 1987 by R. Bruce Bickley, Jr.
Published by the University of Georgia Press
Athens, Georgia 30602
All rights reserved
The paper in this book meets the guidelines for
permanence and durability of the Committee on
Production Guidelines for Book Longevity of the
Council on Library Resources.

Printed in the United States of America

91   90   89   88   87   5   4   3   2   1

Library of Congress Cataloging in Publication Data

Bickley, R. Bruce, 1942–
Joel Chandler Harris.

"Brown thrasher books."
Bibliography: p.
Includes index.
1. Harris, Joel Chandler, 1848–1908.   2. Authors,
American—19th century—Biography.   3. Remus, Uncle
(Fictitious character)   4. Folklore in literature.
5. Afro-Americans in literature.   I. Title.
PS1813.B53   1987   818'.409   [B]   86–16087
ISBN 0-8203-0909-5 (pbk.: alk. paper)

For my daughter Kathryn

Contents

Preface

When Joel Chandler Harris died in 1908, many newspaper editors around the country agreed that he was America's most beloved author. The key to Harris's great popularity was, of course, his Uncle Remus tales, which delighted the common reader because they were genuine yet, at the same time, seemed artless and unsophisticated. Additionally, Harris's stories treated the universals of human experience: children, as well as adults, readily pictured the old black man telling stories to the little boy at his knee; and they laughed just as instinctively as the boy did at Brer Rabbit's wily pranks and roguish style. Partly because of Harris's apparent simplicity and his universality of appeal, discussions of his works have until recently tended to be more appreciative than critically evaluative or scholarly. The one major exception to this pattern is the work of the folklorists, who have been energetically researching origins and analogues for the tar-baby story and other tales for more than nine decades.

Two early biographies of Harris developed the essential facts of his life and character and the background for his work, but neither provided an adequate critical overview of his writings. Robert L. Wiggins's *The Life of Joel Chandler Harris: From Obscurity in Boyhood to Fame in Early Manhood*[1] treats Harris's literary apprenticeship at Turnwold plantation and his early days with the *Atlanta Constitution*. An affectionate biography by Harris's daughter-in-law, Julia Collier Harris, was published the same year as Wiggins's; *The Life and Letters of Joel Chandler Harris*[2] discusses Harris's self-consciousness and diffidence but is chiefly important for its inclusion of unpublished letters and reminiscences of Harris's friends and family. While also appreciative, the most balanced study thus far of Harris's life and works is Paul Cousins's *Joel Chandler Harris: A Biography.*[3] Cousins stresses Harris's retiring personality, his formative years as a printer's assistant, and his generally optimistic vision.

Until a full edition of Harris's letters[4] and a definitive scholarly biography are available, students of Harris will continue to draw upon the work of Wiggins, Julia Collier Harris, and Cousins; and, in preparing my study, I am especially indebted to Cousins's biography. Also helpful in evaluating Harris's writings are Stella Brewer Brookes's *Joel Chandler Harris — Folklorist,*[5] which classifies his folk tales, and a second book by Julia Collier Harris, *Joel Chandler Harris: Editor and Essayist,*[6] which is a useful compilation of his newspaper and magazine articles. Some of the more insightful commentaries about Harris's art and psychological makeup have appeared only in the last ten years or so in a few provocative books about American literary realism and in individual articles.

Since Harris is a much richer and more accomplished author than is generally recognized, this book seeks to analyze his literary artistry and the relationship of his writings to his life more carefully than has previously been done. The study has three major emphases. First, the two beginning chapters review Harris's life, discussing as succinctly as possible the influence of his pathological shyness and reticence on the parameters of his journalistic and literary career. Second, in Chapters 3 through 6 I build upon perspectives established in the first part of the book by examining critically Harris's entire canon and by evaluating his literary craftsmanship, his techniques, and his themes in esthetically related works. Chapter 3 discusses, therefore, the major Uncle Remus volumes; Chapter 4, the later fables and children's books; Chapter 5, his local-color tales, which in many ways were Harris's finest work; and Chapter 6 explores his attempts at novel-writing. In Chapter 7, a general estimate of Harris's vision and importance as a writer is presented. The third emphasis of the book is to offer in the text, in Notes and References, and in the Selected Bibliography, a thorough and up-to-date survey of scholarship and folkloristic research about Harris. I have, however, given particular emphasis to the more significant or suggestive studies; but important appreciative essays are also cited.

As scholars are now discovering, Harris was a more complex and contradictory personality than his contemporaries realized. Furthermore, Harris brought much of this inner complexity into his literary work, which contains more psychological tensions, hidden themes, and rhetorical subtleties than its typically comic or cheerful surface would suggest; to a significant degree, he was trying to come to grips with his own identity in writing his stories and tales. This book attempts to bring the whole Joel Chandler Harris into view.

R. BRUCE BICKLEY, JR.

Florida State University

Acknowledgments

I would especially like to thank Dr. Thomas H. English, former director of the Joel Chandler Harris Collection and professor of English at Emory University, both for his considerable assistance in the past dozen years as I pursued a number of Harris projects, and for his friendship. Professor English's name appears on the title page of many books and monographs on Harris, and in the Acknowledgments section of several more. All Harris scholars are directly or indirectly in his debt, in more ways than we realize.

The Brown Thrasher edition is a reprint of the text of the 1978 Joel Chandler Harris biography but contains an expanded and completely updated annotated secondary bibliography.

Chronology

1848   Joel Chandler Harris born to Mary Harris in Eatonton, Putnam County, Georgia, on December 9.

1856   Begins primary schooling in Eatonton.

1862–   Works as printer's devil for the *Countryman* on Joseph
1866   Addison Turner's plantation, Turnwold; hears plantation fables from old slaves and publishes a few essays, reviews, and poems.

1866–   Typesetter for *Macon Telegraph;* private secretary to William Evelyn of *New Orleans Crescent Monthly.*
1867

1867–   Printer and editor for *Monroe Advertiser* of Forsyth,
1870   Georgia.

1870–   Associate editor of *Savannah Morning News;* marries
1876   Esther LaRose in April 1873.

1876   Becomes associate editor of *Atlanta Constitution;* publishes first Uncle Remus sketch.

1878   *The Romance of Rockville* serialized in *Constitution.*

1880   *Uncle Remus: His Songs and His Sayings.*

1881   Moves to the Wren's Nest, West End Atlanta.

1882   Meets Mark Twain, George Washington Cable, and James Osgood in New Orleans; declines to take part in lecture tour; attends Tile Club dinner, New York City.

1883   *Nights with Uncle Remus.*

1884   *Mingo and Other Sketches in Black and White.*

1886   Visited by A. B. Frost; Henry Grady lectures on "The New South" in New York City.

1887   *Free Joe and Other Georgian Sketches.*

1889   *Daddy Jake the Runaway and Short Stories Told after Dark.*

1891   *Balaam and His Master and Other Sketches and Stories.*

1892   *On the Plantation; Uncle Remus and His Friends.*

1893   *Evening Tales.*

1894   *Little Mr. Thimblefinger and His Queer Country.*

1895   New edition of *Uncle Remus: His Songs and His Sayings* with illustrations by A. B. Frost; *Mr. Rabbit at Home.*

1896   *The Story of Aaron; Stories of Georgia; Sister Jane: Her Friends and Acquaintances;* growing interest in Catholicism.

1897   *Aaron in the Wildwoods.*

1898   *Tales of the Home Folks in Peace and War.*

1899   *Plantation Pageants; The Chronicles of Aunt Minervy Ann.*

1900   *On the Wing of Occasions;* retires from the *Constitution;* James Whitcomb Riley spends two weeks at the Wren's Nest.

1902   *The Making of a Statesman and Other Stories; Gabriel Tolliver: A Story of Reconstruction;* awarded honorary degree by Emory College.

1903   *Wally Wanderoon and His Story-Telling Machine.*

1904   *A Little Union Scout; The Tar-Baby and Other Rhymes of Uncle Remus.*

1905   *Told by Uncle Remus;* elected a member of the American Academy of Arts and Letters; honored by President Theodore Roosevelt in Atlanta.

1907   *Uncle Remus and Brer Rabbit;* visits the White House at Roosevelt's invitation; named editor of *Uncle Remus's Magazine.*

1908   Baptized a Catholic in June; dies of acute nephritis on July 3 in Atlanta.

1909   *The Bishop and the Boogerman; The Shadow Between His Shoulder-Blades.*

1910   *Uncle Remus and the Little Boy.*

1918   *Uncle Remus Returns.*

CHAPTER 1

A Cornfield Journalist

I Boyhood and Literary Apprenticeship

THE circumstances surrounding Joel Chandler Harris's birth had profound effects on both his personality and his art. Joel's mother, Mary Harris, left a respected family in Newton County, Georgia, to move with her lover, an Irish laborer, to Eatonton in nearby Putnam County. They were never married; and, shortly after Joel's birth on December 9, 1848, his father deserted. Joel carried the knowledge of his illegitimacy throughout his life, but he referred to it only obliquely in an occasional comment.[1] Yet illegitimate birth, children abandoned by their fathers, families broken or emotionally scarred, and women who were vigorously independent became persistent motifs in Harris's fiction.

Furthermore, Harris was painfully modest and self-effacing all his life and had a slight speech impediment that could quickly turn into a stammer when he was put on the spot, or forced to take the verbal initiative. He adamantly refused throughout his career to read from his works or to talk informally in front of a group of listeners. In fact, he once wrote Thomas Nelson Page that the self-consciousness he felt "never even gives me a chance to be modest," for he had an "abject horror of making myself conspicuous."[2] During the last half of his life, Harris also stubbornly clung to an old-fashioned style of dress and insisted on wearing a hat indoors when he worked. Psychologists might credit Harris's almost pathological behavior to an emotional shock or discovery in his youth; and the passing years did not appreciably lessen his deep-seated anxiety and insecurity about his public and private self. To a considerable extent, Harris found an identity in his work, and he became in time a celebrated journalist and author. But the self-doubt was always there, and it continually manifested itself in his writings.[3]

Initially, Mary Harris was cast off by her family when she left home, but the people of Eatonton received her kindly, and she herself revealed an admirable adaptability and readiness to support herself and her child. Andrew Reid, one of Eatonton's leading citizens, gave her a small cottage behind his own house for her family, which soon included Mary's mother and grandmother who, relenting, moved to town to help with the new baby. Mary opened a seamstress shop, gave neighbors advice about flower-growing, and set about preparing young Joe, as he was called, for grammar school. Harris had his first exposure to the oral tradition from his mother, who enjoyed telling him stories; and he recalled that his desire to write came from her reading Oliver Goldsmith's *The Vicar of Wakefield* to him as a child. Joe's mother never married; but, in terms of his career, her dependence upon him may have been fortuitous. Joe had to drop out of school and take a steady job since there was no working father in the household; this job determined Harris's life's work.

Joe's first thirteen years were spent in Eatonton in the center of Middle Georgia's "corn and cotton" country. As Paul Cousins emphasizes in his thorough portrait of the culture of the region,[4] at the core of the Middle Georgia social and economic structure were the small farmers of modest means, who worked hard, owned few if any slaves, believed stoutly in individualism, and enjoyed the rich, earthy humor that Augustus Baldwin Longstreet, William Tappan Thompson, Charles Henry Smith ("Bill Arp"), and Richard Malcolm Johnston captured in their writings.[5] Harris in time became the most accomplished of the literary interpreters of the Georgia scene, and the qualities of life that he imbued from his Putnam County upbringing were essential to his art. Throughout his career, Harris recalled proudly the vigorous democratic spirit and the respect for personal rights and identity that the Putnam County folk displayed; and he no doubt reflected with humility upon his mother's kind reception when he spoke of the democracy of his native region.

In 1856, Middle Georgia again befriended the Harris family when Reid generously paid young Joe's tuition at Kate Davidson's school for boys and girls. Short in stature, freckled, and crowned with a shock of bright red hair, Joe proved to be extremely shy and self-conscious when girls were present,[6] which may account in part for his undistinguished performance in the classroom and for his early-acquired habits of truancy. Transferring to the Eatonton Academy for boys later that school year may have alleviated somewhat the shyness problem, but it was evident that Joe was always going to be self-conscious in large groups of his peers or in structured social situations. Not surprisingly, young Harris looked outside the classroom for ways to assert himself, and he is remembered by his companions as a great prankster and mischief-maker. Older boys turned to him for leadership and "style," and apparently they were rarely disappointed.

Indeed, one reason that the mature Harris was such a gifted portrayer of Georgian humor was that he had firsthand participation in its traditions. One market day he panicked some hogs in Eatonton's main street, and the squealing hogs caused all the horses in town to pull their ties and bolt. Like Huck Finn, Joe and his friends often "borrowed" melons and peaches from the neighbors' fields, but Joe's favorite sport was stealing Harvey Dennis's pedigreed foxhounds for a good afternoon's rabbit hunt; and Dennis, who learned to indulge the boys, later let them assist in small ways on the big fox-hunts. It was characteristic of Harris that, when the older Hut Adams organized a group of the boys into the "Gully Minstrels," Joe was the "funny man" who clowned with a fiddle.

Throughout his life Harris maintained his Georgian and Irish sense of humor privately as well as publicly, and he was especially fond of well-executed practical jokes. As a perceptive *New York Times* interviewer once observed, Harris's particular kind of humor may have been in part the result of his own innate bashfulness, "very much as an awkward boy falls into witticisms and practical jokes to hide his confusion."[7] Moreover, it suited Harris's own reticent nature that a good practical joke could be arranged ahead of time and its perpetrator concealed from view when the victim came along. As a journalist writing humorous and satirical paragraphs for the *Savannah Morning News,* or daily editorials for the *Constitution* that were designed to educate the public out of its prejudices, Harris could also hide effectively behind his pen; for he thus kept himself at a distance from "the crowd" and was relatively safe from face-to-face confrontations, which always made him terribly nervous.

Harris began his professional life as the recorder of some of the lighter and more humorous facets of the passing scene, and he insisted to the end of his career that he was only a "cornfield chronicler."[8] Yet Harris also saw humor in broader perspective, as an index of one's cultural heritage and character. "The forms of humor that are preserved in the oral literature of the people," Harris wrote in his next-to-last year, "are very dear to them, and for the best of reasons. It is based on their unique experiences; it is a part of their personality; it belongs to their history; and it seems, in some ways, to be an assurance of independence and strength, of sanity and wisdom, of honesty and simplicity."[9] For Harris, in other words, cultivating a sense of humor helped maintain strength and, more important, sanity.

After school, Joe often dropped by the Eatonton post office to read the *Milledgeville Recorder* and the *Milledgeville Federal Union*. With the outbreak of the Civil War, he probably came by even more frequently to read the battle dispatches and to follow as best he could the political debates of the times. As the mood of Eatonton grew more serious with the war's spread southward, so too did the tone of Joe's life change. He was too young to join the Confederate army, but he wanted to do something constructive to help relieve the burden on his mother's shoulders. Then on March 11, 1862, both Milledgeville papers carried notices that Joseph Addison Turner, owner of Turnwold plantation, about nine miles east of town, had started a weekly newspaper, the *Countryman*. When the first issue arrived a few days later, Joe looked through it and found the advertisement that shaped the course of his life: "Wanted: An active, intelligent white boy, 14 or 15 years of age to learn the printer's trade." Harris had already met Turner, for his mother had done some tailoring for him; and, since the door seemed partially ajar, Joe applied for the position. As soon as Turner verified that young Harris had written the letter of application with his own hand, he was hired as a printer's devil.

Joe's four years at Turnwold from March 1862 to May 1866 were so formative that we could never really overestimate their significance. By today's standards, this period would amount at the very least to four years at a liberal-arts college, simultaneous with four years of work in a professional field. Like Benjamin Franklin, Walt Whitman, Mark Twain, and William Dean Howells, Harris began his career as a man of letters by inking type and pulling on a press, looking meanwhile for a chance to get some of his own work in print. For the tutoring in the liberal arts as well as for the technical training, apprentice Harris could not have found a better master than Turner. As Cousins has indicated, Turner was an enterprising, independent-minded planter whose chief ambition was to be a literary man; by the age of thirty-five, he had already taught school, practiced law, served in the Georgia legislature, acquired an English and Classical library of over a thousand volumes, and published at his own expense three books of Romantic poetry and four short-lived literary magazines.[10] However, in editing the *Countryman* for four successful years Turner found a greater measure of satisfaction than he had experienced in any other endeavor, and young Harris was there to share his enthusiasm.

Harris admired Turner as he had admired no other man, and he must have seen him, in part, as the father he had never had. To be sure, Cousins reminds us, not all of the influences that Turner had on Joe were positive ones. Turner's fierce sectionalism, both political and literary, and his devotion to the plantation ideal conditioned Harris's thinking for a considerable time. Yet the Turnwold years gave him not only invaluable professional experience and some badly needed self-confidence but also an artistic heritage that was richer than he realized. In fact, the Turnwold setting took such a firm hold on Harris's memory that it figured in his stories and sketches for the next forty years.

The thousand-acre plantation, which Turner had purchased in 1851, was forested with oak, sycamore, hickory, and pine; and the acreage spread over rolling hills that in places climbed up to Bermuda meadows two hundred feet above the creeks and the red-clay gullies that meandered through the area. The plantation was alive with game, and Harris enthusiastically recalls in his autobiographical narrative *On the Plantation* not only the coon- and fox-hunting expeditions with the older men but also the rabbit hunts that he and fifteen-year-old Jim Polk Gaither experienced.[11] Behind the plain but spacious plantation house was a spring, which is especially prominent in the later Mr. Thimblefinger stories; yet the slave quarters to the west of the house, and the kitchen in the back, drew Joe night after night for long chimney-corner visits with Uncle George Terrell, Old Harbert, and Aunt Crissy, the Turner slaves who were the prototypes for Uncle Remus, Aunt Tempy, and other figures.

Turnwold is still occupied today, although a full-length porch and white columns have been added across the front of the house and much of the original forest land has been cleared for dairy pasturage. But the image of the plantation house, with its driveway lined with trees that Turner himself planted, its scattered outbuildings, and the beautiful vista across the hills that roll gently to the horizon, strikes the eye today as impressively as it must have struck Harris's in 1862.

When Joe arrived for work, Turner was less involved with corn- and cotton-planting than he was with his latest literary venture, the *Countryman*, and with another enterprise that he had begun with the outbreak of hostilities — the manufacturing of felt hats for the Confederate army. Although Turner had been a political independent, he remained loyal to Georgia when she seceded; and he helped the Southern cause as energetically as he could with his newspaper, as well as with his hat factory. As it developed, the Civil War only reinforced Turner's prejudice for Southern authors and his own private ambition to leave his own mark as a respected Southern writer. The irony is that Turner's new apprentice, Joel Chandler Harris, would "accomplish for literature in the South what Turner had dreamed of doing, but without the narrow sectional prejudices and geographical limitations which the latter had prescribed for it."[12]

One of the reasons that the pupil surpassed the master may be that Harris made better use of Turner's advice than did Turner himself. First of all, Turner encouraged the reclusive young boy to read widely in the plantation library during his leisure hours, and he often recommended particular volumes for study. In later years, Harris spoke of his fondness for Chaucer, Dickens, and Sir Thomas Browne, all of whom Turner collected in his library; but Turner's holdings in other major English and Classical authors must also have helped instill in Harris a feeling for the universal themes which constitute great literature. In addition to the Grimms' tales and *The Arabian Nights,* Harris had ready access to works by Shakespeare, Milton, Swift, Addison and Steele, Pope, Thackeray, Emerson, and other major figures; and Turner of course made sure that Joe paid special attention to such important Southern writers as Edgar Allan Poe and Henry Timrod. While he was at Turnwold, Harris's early literary efforts show a strong influence from Poe's quarter, as I shall demonstrate; but Harris's ability to universalize his Southern heritage is what gives the Remus stories and so many of the later local-color tales an enduring place in world literature.

The second lesson that Joe learned from his teacher was that humor has a definite place in journalism. Turner interspersed anecdotes, puns, and witty asides among the articles in the *Countryman* as a way of sharing his heritage of Georgia humor with his readers. Given his own flair for the comic, Harris quickly identified with this kind of journalism and was soon submitting short punning questions and answers to Turner for inclusion in the paper. Although most of these juvenile efforts seem a little strained, Harris was at least learning to flex his journalistic muscles. In the issue for April 14, 1863, the "Countryman's Devil" asks, "Why do the Yankees delay their attack upon the chief Rebel port?" His response: "Because they find a Charles*ton* too heavy for their gunboats to *carry.*"[13] Soon local newspapermen among Turner's two thousand subscribers began to notice the "Devil's" puns and to respond with their own.

While Joe was setting type for the *Countryman* and printing his own short pieces when he could, he had the unique experience of having Turner revise galley proof for style and focus while he quite literally watched over his shoulder. The first time Harris submitted an article to the *Countryman* Turner refused to publish it, and responded instead with an open letter, "To a Young Correspondent," printed in the paper on October 27, 1862. In his letter Turner counseled the fledgling journalist to compress his language and to curb his "exuberant fancy." Above all, "study simplicity and artlessness of style.... You have a talent for writing, and I advise you to cultivate it." And then Turner closed with a characteristic reminder: "There is a glorious field just ahead of you for Southern writers." In correcting Harris's own galley sheets, Turner illustrated graphically the lessons he sought to teach his apprentice.

From December 1862 through the spring of 1866 Harris published more than thirty items in the *Countryman* that can be identified as his work, as well as at least one brief moral tale in a Georgia religious periodical. His earliest writings were primarily the short humorous queries, along with reflective essays on subjects varying from "A Sabbath Evening in the Country" to "The Progress of Civilization." Harris's most learned writing is found in his book reviews of the romantic poetry by the Macon writer Henry Lynden Flash; of a novel by the Alabama authoress Augusta Evans; and of Rufus Griswold's biography of Poe. But, during his years at Turnwold, Harris's real ambition was to be a poet, and he published at least a dozen poems in the *Countryman*. Although he experimented with various stanzaic forms, including the sonnet, he worked hardest, it seems, to achieve the melancholy strains and images that Poe sought in his poems about "the most poetical topic in the world," the death of a beautiful woman.

In "Moselle," "Our Minne Grey," "Mary," "Nelly White," and "Moonlight," Harris treats the separation of lovers, followed by the death of the loved one, or the lover's memories of his lost soul-mate that are recalled by a visit to her grave. Perhaps the most sincere of these poems is "Mary," which Harris may have written in praise of his mother. The last two stanzas deserve quoting:

> Like echoes of the mermaids' sigh,
> Or of the ocean's swell,
> Which poets say forever hide
> Within the bright sea shell,
> Thy image in my inmost heart
> Will ever fondly dwell.
>
> Thou art my thoughts each weary day,
> My dreaming all the night,
> And still I see thy gentle smile
> And hear thy footstep light —
> But tears are gathering in my eyes;
> I cannot see to write.

More psychologically poignant is "Accursed," a poem recounting a woman's seduction, her abandonment by her lover, and her death following the birth of her child. "The woman was weak, but pure and good," writes Harris, but "In the heart of the man was *sin*." The poem closes with an image that Harris must have fantasized more than once when he reflected upon his and his mother's betrayal by his unfaithful father: the man commits suicide, overcome at last by despair and the "curse" of his sin. Harris's earliest literary works, and, as I shall indicate, much of the writing to come, were inextricably tied to his own psychological history.

While he was composing his own verse and favorably reviewing Flash's now-forgotten poetry, Harris conceived his first major literary project: a collection of Southern verse accompanied by biographical and critical sketches of the anthologized poets. Newspaper clippings and letters from the Turnwold days and from the two-year period that followed reveal that Harris was planning a collection of some fifty-one authors, probably to be entitled "Gems of Southern Poetry"; it is obvious that Turner's fervor for Southern letters was affecting the impressionable Harris. Although the young writer never brought his project to completion, some of the fruits of his labor may have seen their way into print nevertheless. Harris had corresponded about his plans with James Wood Davidson, and his *Living Writers of the South* (1869) may have made use of some of Harris's critical and biographical material.[14] In any case, Davidson published in his collection two poems that Harris had written in 1867.

The informal part of Harris's education at Turnwold is more difficult to document, but it was the more significant half in terms of the literary and folkloristic legacy that it bestowed upon Harris, and, through him, upon us. Joel had considerable free time between issues of the newspaper for exploring the plantation and for getting to know Turner's three children, his overseer, his other workers in the print shop and factory, and his household and field slaves. Turner had to borrow heavily to keep his several enterprises going, and the accounts Cousins has reviewed show that Turnwold was run as a relatively benevolent and humane operation. Even at the height of Turner's proslavery editorializing in the *Countryman,* he was encouraging economic independence among his twenty-five hands by paying them for extra crops that they grew on land he had given them, and by selling for them any tools and farm implements that they made. Old Harbert and some of the other slaves remained so committed to Turner that, after the Civil War, they stayed at Turnwold.

Harris spent hundreds of hours in the "quarters" during his years at Turnwold, and he was often joined by Turner's son Joseph Sidney and by his two daughters. Joel felt less self-conscious around the patient and indulgent older slaves; and, as Jay B. Hubbell suggests, his own humble background probably gave him insight into the mind of the black field hand.[15] Furthermore, his supersensitivity to people also found a new, and healthier, direction: he listened with a keen ear for inflection, and with an eye for gesture, to the dialectical and narrative rhythms, the humor, and the irony of the animal fables that Terrell and other Negroes shared with him. Harris learned to love these folk tales. Moreover, at Turnwold an image became fixed in Joe's consciousness: that of a wise old Negro who was educating a young white boy about the black race's folk heritage, but who was also finding opportunities to give him moral counsel or to chastise him whenever his mischievousness became too insistent. Last but not least, Uncle George Terrell and Old Harbert, who are represented in the composite folk character Uncle Remus, may, like Turner himself, have helped fill the place of the absent father in Harris's life.

Despite Turner's shaky financial base, he was able to continue his operations a year beyond the fall of the Confederacy in the spring of 1865. But the collapse of the old plantation system was both economic and psychological reason enough for Turner to suspend publication of the *Countryman* on May 8, 1866. Although the Turnwold years proved to be the happiest and most carefree of Joe's life, he had no choice but to return to Eatonton. When he left Turnwold, neither he nor his defeated mentor realized that vested in the person of the *Countryman*'s printer's devil was the most authentic vision of life on the old plantation that American literature would ever see.

II   *The Road to Atlanta*

Harris came back to Eatonton in the spring of 1866 with little money in his pocket but with considerable experience to show for his years at Turnwold. After a brief homecoming with his mother, Harris accepted an offer of a typesetting job with the *Macon Telegraph,* which was owned and edited by a former Eatontonian. As Cousins observes, the *Telegraph* position was attractive to Harris because of the forty-mile proximity of Macon to Eatonton and because the paper, which had been supporting the cause of Southern letters, seemed to afford him additional opportunity for serious literary composition. As it turned out, Joe's five or six months with the *Telegraph,* from May to October or November 1867, were lively enough but did not bring him the kind of professional experience he sought. The staff of the *Telegraph,* from the city editor Harry Neville down through the printers' assistants, enjoyed pranks and beer-drinking more than literature. While everyone had to work harder than Harris ever had on the *Countryman* to get out the daily issues, the vogue for personalized journalism and humor that was prevalent in newspaper-writing from New York to Clemens's Virginia City, Nevada, spilled over continually into the staff's routine. Harris's red hair, self-consciousness, and stammering, always more severe when older white men were present, became subjects for jest in the office and even in Neville's columns. The joking may at times have irritated the diffident Joe Harris, but he found that drinking the tavern brew with the staff was relaxing, if not indeed therapeutic.

In addition to setting type, Joe reviewed books and journals and composed humorous or complimentary "puffs" that thanked local merchants for gifts to the staff. He continued to write poetry; but, as he did not receive much encouragement to publish what he considered his best literary work, he not surprisingly began to look elsewhere for a more promising position. One of the newer magazines that Joe had been reviewing enthusiastically was the New Orleans *Crescent Monthly,* which was published by William Evelyn, who advertised that his magazine was "Devoted to Literature, Art, Science, and Society," and that it sought to rise above mere sectionalism by publishing only those works that merited it. If Southern literature was to prove itself worthy of a permanent place in American letters, Evelyn advised that now was the chance for the Southern writer to show his capabilities. Although the details are sketchy, Joe apparently accepted Evelyn's principles as a kind of challenge and wrote to him about a job. He must have been somewhat surprised to receive in the return mail an offer to be Evelyn's personal secretary. After some deliberation Harris accepted and moved to New Orleans in the fall of 1866.

As the months passed, Joe realized that this job, too, was not helping him become a more accomplished writer. Furthermore, to a pathologically shy boy from rural Putnam the overwhelming size of New Orleans and its overlay of languages and cultural strains made it seem a veritable foreign country. Joe so respected Evelyn that he later named one of his children after him, but nothing appeared over Joe's signature in the *Crescent Monthly.* The *New Orleans Times* did publish two of his poems; but, since Joe felt no real incentive to apply himself to literary work, he resigned from his position in May 1867 to return to the familiar landscape of his native state.

Happy to be home again, Joe quickly accepted an offer to be an "editor" with the *Monroe Advertiser* of Forsyth, Georgia. Owned by James P. Harrison, who had once worked for Turner's *Countryman,* the weekly *Advertiser* was a paper of small circulation, and professionally Joe took a step down the ladder in working for Harrison. The *Advertiser* only carried local news, but eighteen-year-old Harris, who by now must have realized that his plans for a literary career were a little premature, spent three enjoyable years performing the standard chores that his position required: "I set all the type, pulled the press, kept the books, swept the floor, and wrapped the papers for mailing; my mechanical, accounting, and menial duties being concealed from the vulgar hilarity of the world outside Forsyth by the honorable and impressive title of *Editor*."[16]

It is ironic that, by relaxing into his work at Forsyth, Harris achieved the kind of visibility that would eventually earn him an important position with the South's major newspaper and a place in the front ranks of Southern writers. After a year or so in Forsyth, Joe had abandoned his "Gems of Southern Poetry" project; although he wrote an occasional poem, he found that composing humorous paragraphs for the *Advertiser* about Georgia life and character was satisfying as well as entertaining work. His Turnwold puns had been a start in this direction, but the Georgia newspapers began to give Harris's paragraphs wide coverage, and he was suddenly in the limelight. Harris also wrote a series of sketches and stories about Georgia fox-hunting for the *Advertiser* that gained him some attention.

The Forsyth years were also important ones for another reason, for Joe learned during this period to share something of his private self and inner anxieties with another person. Joe lived in the home of James Harrison, the *Advertiser's* owner; he soon developed a close friendship with Harrison's sister, Mrs. Georgia Starke, and Mrs. Starke's young daughter Nora Belle quickly became Joe's favorite "little fairy." The candor, geniality, and good sense of Mrs. Starke encouraged Joe to speak of his self-consciousness, and in Joe's letters to her after he had left Forsyth he mentioned his unfortunate past and the discomfort that his "morbidly sensitive" nature, his "*absolute horror* of strangers" (Harris's emphasis), and his "awkwardness and clumsiness" so often caused him.[17] Georgia Starke tried to give Joe more self-confidence and to reinforce his desire to become a better writer; at the very least, her friendship helped him accept himself and believe that in time he would gain the status he deserved as an author. Their relationship proved to be an enduring one; for, when Mrs. Starke and her daughter later moved to Atlanta, Harris and his family often visited them; and Joe frequently recalled Georgia's patience and "unfailing kindness" and corresponded with her until just before his death.

Forsyth was the real turning point in Harris's life; for, as Wiggins observes, "the youth became the man."[18] Joel not only learned the meaning of adult friendship and matured emotionally but more realistically evaluated his own abilities and turned, for the moment at least, more deliberately toward a career as a "cornfield" journalist. Then in the fall of 1870 his new profession as a humorous paragrapher suddenly reaped an unexpected reward: he received an offer to be an associate editor of the *Savannah Morning News,* one of the state's most respected papers, for the unheard-of salary of forty dollars a week. Harris left so quickly for Savannah that he literally did not have time to pack his trunk, and his printing assistant shipped it later.

In a sense Harris's move to the *Morning News* was a coming-home to a heritage of Georgia humor. The founder and, in the 1870s, the editor of the paper was William Tappan Thompson, whose Major Jones sketches were second only to A. B. Longstreet's *Georgia Scenes* in regional popularity. Harris's humorous paragraphing for the *News,* which had already earned him a state-wide reputation, would soon make his name a commonplace in the Southeast as well. Harris enjoyed his sudden prestige and, doing his best to enter into the spirit of things, frequently joked with the staff, who nicknamed him "Red-Top," "Pink-Top," and "Vermilion Pate." When his paragraphs from his "Affairs in Georgia" column were reprinted around the state, they were labeled "Harris Sparks," "Red-Top Flashes," "Hot shots from Red Hair-is," and the like.

Some of Harris's paragraphs suggest the stock-in-trade jokes and the one-liners of the stand-up comedians who have been part of the American scene for the last century or more: "A suffrage-slinger in Rome named Sam Rambo recently caressed his wife with a panful of fire-coals. The authorities of that city have gone so far as to put Sam in jail. This country is coming to a pretty pass when a free American citizen can't amuse himself with his own wife." Racial and ethnic slurs have always been a part of humor, and Harris's work in this vein was generally tasteful: "The colored people of Macon celebrated the birthday of Lincoln again on Wednesday. This is the third time since last October." "A colored couple in Putnam County whose combined age is one hundred and eighty-two years, were united in wedlock recently. They said the reason they were so precipitate about the thing, they didn't want their parents to find out." Versions of this joke are still in circulation today.

But in weaker moments, Harris catered to some of the standard Southern prejudices: "A Lumpkin negro seriously injured his pocketknife recently by undertaking to stab a colored brother in the head." Even after he became a nationally known author, Harris still tended to lapse into overt racial humor. In working with Harris's unpublished letters, Joseph M. Griska has learned that

Harris's racial joking continued past 1885. And, Arlin Turner has informed me, the Huntington Library manuscript of "Little Compton," a Civil War tale published in *Century* before Harris gathered it in *Free Joe and Other Georgian Sketches* (1887), originally contained an episode in which a master threatened to whip his absentminded black servant. The *Century's* Richard Watson Gilder tactfully edited out the episode.

Harris relaxed and put on weight in Savannah. On April 23, 1873, the *News's* biggest rival, the *Atlanta Constitution,* which had been reprinting Harris's paragraphs since his Forsyth days, could not refrain from publishing a humorous but highly complimentary genealogical sketch of "Jinks Conundrum Harris." They compared Joe Harris favorably to Rabelais, Falstaff, and Twain and then noted: "Harris exudes, drools, eats, breathes, looks, imagines, and gesticulates humor. He, indeed, murmurs jokes, even in the tender hours of love, 'which the same' he is very fond of. But we must stop. The very suggestion of Harris sets our paper capering with laughter, our table to cutting up didoes, our pen to dancing a sort of Highland fling."

As Cousins suggests, the kind of humor that Harris, Twain, Artemus Ward, and others were indulging in during the Reconstruction era brought a form of comic relief to the South. For Harris personally, his success as Georgia's leading "funny man" helped him gain confidence, but he also began to develop a reputation as an editorial writer. Harris's editorials of the 1870s reveal not only his impatience with shady morality and with "shifty" politicians but also his democratic philosophy and humanitarianism; and these themes he iterated in newspaper and magazine columns all of his life.[19]

While Harris's career was on the rise, romance entered his life. Joe, who had been residing at the Florida House since his arrival in Savannah, had become well acquainted with Captain and Mrs. Pierre LaRose, French-Canadians formerly of Quebec; Captain LaRose, it developed, owned a steamer that plied the Georgia and North Florida coasts. The LaRoses' buoyant and attractive seventeen-year-old daughter, Esther, graduated from the Catholic convent school in St. Hyacinthe, Quebec, and joined her family at the Florida House in early 1872. Joel's shy and self-effacing personality was by no means transformed by Essie, but she gave his life stability. The diary and poetry he mailed to Essie after she returned to Canada that summer show the depth of his love; and, when she responded in kind, they arranged a quiet marriage in Savannah on Sunday evening, April 20, 1873. Published letters and reminiscences suggest that a peaceful home life and children at his knee provided the psychological still point around which Harris's journalistic career could turn, although he was never free from his neuroses. The Harrises had two children by the fall of 1876 and seven more followed, but illness took three of their offspring at an early age.[20] Essie was a devout Catholic. While not a churchgoer, Joel nevertheless had strong religious convictions; and Essie's strength of faith so impressed him that, shortly before his death, he joined the Catholic Church.

In August 1876 a vicious yellow fever epidemic hit Savannah. There would have been no reason for the Harrises to leave the area otherwise, for Joel could not hope for a better salary; but in early September they took little Julian and Lucien to the higher ground and more healthy atmosphere of Atlanta to wait for the epidemic to subside. Joel characteristically kept his sense of humor through the ordeal, as his registration entry at the Kimball House suggests: "J. C. Harris, one wife, two bowlegged children, and a bilious nurse." Harris had been in Atlanta a little over a month when Evan Howell, editor of the prestigious *Constitution,* and Howell's new associate editor, Henry W. Grady — who had met Harris in 1871 when Grady was editor of the *Rome Commercial* — offered the man whose work they had both so long admired a temporary position on the paper. Although the epidemic had waned in Savannah, the economic confusion that it had produced in the city made it impossible for Thompson to bring Harris back at his old salary. In short order, Joe was hired permanently at the *Constitution* at twenty-five dollars a week for editorial paragraphing, plus an additional five dollars for being telegraph editor. The final and most successful phase of Harris's career as a journalist had begun, but Harris and his public were yet to discover his latent abilities as a folklorist, a social historian, and a literary artist.

III   *The* Constitution *and a Literary Awakening*

Harris arrived in Atlanta just as the city was beginning its second decade of phenomenal recovery and growth after its destruction in 1864. Atlanta's population had jumped from 9,554 to 21,789 between 1860 and 1870, and most of the increase had occurred after the Civil War and had been accelerated by the city's being declared the state capital in 1868. By 1880 her population had climbed to 37,409, making her the fastest-growing city in the Southeast.[21] Enthusiasm, optimism about the future, and civic pride pervaded Atlanta in the 1870s; and Harris imbibed as much of this atmosphere as possible, partly because he was stimulated by it and partly as therapy for his own introspectiveness and latent insecurity.

The *Constitution,* which had been founded the same year Atlanta became the capital, had become by 1876 the city's leading paper and a major voice in the Southeast. With the acquisition of Grady and Harris as associate editors, the *Constitution* had a one-two editorial punch that soon brought the paper national recognition and influence. Grady became the outspoken advocate of the economic and political cooperation of the South with the North in order to create a reconstituted "New South" of industry and business, and Harris more temperately but no less effectively demonstrated in his editorials and in his art the qualities of mind and life in agrarian Southern culture that could ease the pains of war and help effect a renaissance of Southern letters.

From the start, Grady saw his role clearly and championed his Southern cause; but Harris found his real strength as a writer almost accidentally. He had begun to compose a column of humorous paragraphs to be called "Roundabout in Georgia," but the resignation of Sam W. Small from the staff left a small vacuum which Harris was asked to fill. Small had been contributing a series of dialect sketches featuring observations on the local scene by Old Si, an Atlanta Negro. The sketches had been popular; and, when Howell asked Harris to try his hand at them, Harris wrote two, employing the black dialect that he had heard as a boy in Putnam County. Both "Markham's Ball" and "Jeems Robinson" appeared in the *Constitution* on October 26, 1876 — the same issue, in fact, that carried Harris's initial "Roundabout in Georgia" column.

The first sketch, "Markham's Ball," was a slight one that consisted of old Uncle Ben's humorous comments about a local political celebration; however, "Jeems Robinson," as Cousins says, "bore the stamp of Harris' genius."[22] A seemingly effortless piece of writing, it was carefully structured. A young Jonesboro Negro and an older man are passing the time of day at the train station when the younger man inquires about " 'Jeems Rober'son,' " whom he had not seen " 'sence he cut loose fum de chain-gang. . . . He ain't down wid de biliousness, is he?' " The older man responds casually that Jim has not been sick; he had just tried to ride Mars John's cantankerous roan mule and " 'de mule, she up'n do like she got nudder ingagement.' " Then the older speaker, fully aware of the rhetorical leverage that he has over his listener, looks around and says it is time for the young man to catch his train. Naturally, the Jonesboro man wants the rest of the story, so the older man acknowledges that there had, in fact, been a scuffle. When the dust cleared, Jim lay on the ground, and the mule stood at the trough with Jim's suspenders wrapped around her back legs. " 'Den atterwuds, de ker'ner, he come 'round, an' he tuck'n gin it out dat Jim died sorter accidental like.' " Then the old man adds with a subtle rhetorical twist: " 'Hit's des like I tell you: de nigger wern't sick a minnit.' "

Four years later, Harris collected his second sketch as the first of Uncle Remus's "Sayings" in *Uncle Remus: His Songs and His Sayings;* at that time, the piece is given a more ironic title, "Jeems Rober'son's Last Illness," and the old man is identified as "Uncle Remus." But, for all practical purposes, Harris discovered in this sketch not only Remus as narrator but also the power of the vernacular, which Joel wrote easily and instinctively. As Twain said the dialect humorist should do,[23] Harris's storyteller never indicates that anything funny exists in what he is saying, and he knows how to use a pause effectively. Moreover, the Uncle Remus prototype thoroughly understands human nature. In this 300-word sketch, an important new voice becomes part of the tradition of American humor and storytelling.

A character simply named "Remus" has a minor role in Harris's sketch "Politics and Provisions" printed on October 31, 1876; but not until November 28 did "Uncle Remus" begin to appear as a regular figure in the *Constitution.* J. T. Manry, who had been Harris's assistant during his days on the *Monroe Advertiser* in Forsyth, recalls that the postmaster's gardener was named "Uncle Remus" and that Joel had found the name appealing. Whatever the origin of the name, Harris acknowledged later that Uncle Remus was not his own invention but was instead a "human syndicate" of three or four black men he had known.[24] It is important to note, however, that while Uncle George Terrell and Old Harbert from Harris's Turnwold days were recreated in the Uncle Remus character that is most familiar to us — the plantation storyteller and rural philosopher — the first Uncle Remus was an old Atlanta Negro, formerly from the country, who liked to drop by the *Consti-*

tution's editorial room. The urban Uncle Remus displayed the storytelling gifts that his Putnam County cousin used so effectively, but his character and his pet subjects were somewhat different. In sketches like "Uncle Remus's Politics," "Turnip Salad as a Subject," and "Race Improvement," the Atlanta Remus complains about his troubles, and he chastises politicians for their ineffectuality and slick city Negroes for their willingness to take a dole from the government, or to steal a neighbor's chicken, instead of doing an honest day's work. As Thomas English points out, Harris retained the Atlanta Remus for use in commenting on the Reconstruction scene and the city Negroes' "thin veneer of culture"; and he used him even while he was developing the Remus from down in Putnam. He saw no reason to try to reconcile the two figures, but in time the Atlanta Remus was subordinated to the rural storyteller.[25]

The first portrait we have of the Old South, plantation Remus is suggested only indirectly in "Uncle Remus's Revival Hymn," published in the *Constitution* on January 18, 1877. Widely reprinted in papers around the country, the hymn asks the old question about being ready when judgment day comes. Uncle Remus gives his audience the only possible answer in the fourth stanza:

> De time is right now an' dis here's de place —
> Let de salvashun sun shine squar' in yo' face,
> Fight de battles uv de Lord, fight soon an' fight late,
> An' you'll allers fine a latch to de goldin' gate.

Harris's recreation of this old-time hymn, and of other plantation songs in subsequent issues, apparently brought to his mind other warm recollections of his plantation experiences. When Sam Small temporarily rejoined the *Constitution* in early 1877 and resumed his "Old Si" sketches, Harris began writing a series of reminiscent essays and narratives about rural life for the Sunday edition of the paper. His subjects ranged from "The Cornfield Pea" and "A Georgia Fox Hunt" to "A Country Newspaper," "The Old Plantation," and "A Country Church"; and he was discovering in all of these that his Putnam and Turnwold years had left him a considerable legacy.

Harris reveals his increasing interest in placing Uncle Remus in a plantation setting in "Uncle Remus as a Rebel," published in October 1877. Printed in a revised version as "A Story of the War" in the first Remus volume, this work was his most ambitious piece of fiction to date. It illustrates not only Harris's increasing maturity as a literary artist but also two of the "public" themes that dominated his stories and novels for the next thirty years: his belief in human dignity, and the need for reconciliation between North and South. In this story, Remus relates in dialect his war experience down in " 'Putmon' " County after his young " 'Mars Jeems' " had left to fight the approaching Yankees. After the plantation overseer had been conscripted, Remus was put in charge of the place. Loyal to his " 'Ole Miss' " and to her daughter Miss Sally, Jeems's sister, Remus calmly stands by them with his ax ready as Yankees enter the house.

The story focuses on Remus's instinctive actions when a Union sharpshooter tries to shoot Mars Jeems, who had returned to the area one afternoon: Remus kills the Yankee, even though the soldier is fighting for Remus's freedom. In the revised story, the Yankee soldier, John Huntingdon, simply loses an arm to his wounds; and, after Remus and Miss Sally nurse him back to health, John and Sally are married. When the Huntingdons later move to Atlanta, Remus accompanies them; and, as he explains to one of John's relatives who protests that Remus had cost John an arm, " 'I gin 'im dem,' " pointing to Mrs. Huntingdon, " 'en I gin 'im deze,' " indicating his own two arms. " 'En ef dem ain't nuff fer enny man den I done los' de way.' "

Earlier in his story, Remus had muttered to John that he was tired of life in Atlanta, especially of " 'deze yer sunshine niggers' " that borrowed his tools, begged his tobacoo, and stole his "vittles." " 'I gotter pack up en go,' " he concluded. " 'I'm agwine down ter Putmon, dat's w'at.' " More than a year passed before Harris effected Remus's relocation, but this initial work at recreating fictionally an old-time Negro and the white society around him anticipated the fuller portraits of blacks and whites to come.

Although deadlines were always hanging over Harris's head, his work for the *Constitution* continued to prove congenial; and, as had been the case in Macon and Savannah, practical joking and "funning" were natural parts of Atlanta journalism. In the summer of 1878, for example, some wag on the staff wrote a broadside mock-epic of several stanzas that celebrated Harris's red hair; written appropriately in red ink, the poem wittily recounts an attempt by the local fire brigade to quench Joel's "flaming" hair. When its efforts prove futile, the poet observes that Harris needs no chandelier to light his desk, for his burning skull is sufficient illumination; in fact, Joel might charitably offer to be either a lamp-post to light the way of drunken men or a lighthouse to warn ships of dangerous shoals.[26] During his later Atlanta years, Harris may have decided that his carrot-red hair was no longer a fit subject for jest. Joseph Griska has speculated in a letter to me that Harris's habit of wearing a hat indoors was in part a defensive reaction to the incessant joking about his hair.

When Sam Small left the paper for the last time in March 1878, Harris contributed more Atlanta Remus sketches and another plantation song, but he also tried his hand for the first time at the novel form. *The Romance of Rockville,* serialized in the *Weekly Constitution* from April 16 through September 24, 1878, is discussed more fully in Chapter 6, but it is important to note here that Harris was already working to expand the scope of his literary vision. Harris was always proud to call himself a "Cracker," and the plot of the novel and its portrait of prewar lower- and middle-class Georgia society anticipate by some eighteen years another, more ambitious book on Georgia life, *Sister Jane.* It is also psychologically significant that the theme of Harris's initial attempt at extended narrative is the restoration of an orphaned boy to his family. As had been the case with his poetry, from the earliest days of his fiction-writing Harris's personal history was bound up with his art.

While he was following his artistic and literary impulses and experimenting with the story and novel, the "public" Harris, the journalist, wrote daily copy and contributed signed editorials to the Sunday *Constitution.* Harris wrote in 1878 that there "never was a time when an editor with a purpose could accomplish more for his state and his country than just at present. What a legacy for one's conscience to know that one has been instrumental in mowing down the old prejudices that rattle in the wind like weeds."[27] Throughout his career as a journalist, Harris worked to rid the reading public of its three "old prejudices": social and political sectionalism, literary sectionalism, and racial intolerance. In evaluating today Harris's vision as a New South editor, we must

always remember that he was writing from a late nineteenth-
century perspective, not a late twentieth-century one, and that his
opinions were progressive for his day even if they fall short of the
liberal thinking of our own time.

Harris's point of view toward the problem of social and political
sectionalism often parallels his line of argument about provincialism in literature. In essays written during 1879 and 1880, Harris felt
that the North, more than the South, was delaying the reconciliation of the two halves of the country; if the North were sending
some able, unprovincial, and humane Republican officials to work
with Southern leaders, rather than carpetbaggers and political self-
seekers, the nation could move forward more peacefully. Although
the Southerners were by no means guiltless of the kind of provincialism so often shown by the North, the charges of reprisals, personal or political, against the Negro, or of the Southern obstruction
of Union law, could often be traced to the machinations of the federal agents themselves.

A similar theme runs through two characteristic literary editorials of the same period. "The very spice and essence of all literature," Harris wrote in "Literature in the South" on November 30,
1879, "is localism. No literary artist can lack for materials in this
section." Hence, "In literature, art and society, whatever is truly
Southern is likewise truly American; and the same may be said of
what is truly Northern." Mere sectionalism in literature is destruc-
tive, but "the flavor of localism" graces real literary art. Harris's
editorial is a warning to all writers, the Southern artist not
excepted. Southerners feel they must praise the "sickening dog-
gerel" of "Miss Sweetie Wildwood" because she happens to be the
daughter of Colonel Wildwood. "What is the result? Why, simply
this, that the stuff we are in the habit of calling Southern literature
is not only a burlesque upon literary art, but a humiliation and a
disgrace to the people whose culture it is supposed to represent."

Harris again looks at the problem of sectionalism, from a Northern perspective, in "Provinciality in Literature—A Defense of Boston" on January 25, 1880. Suggesting that Boston can learn a
lesson from Atlanta, Harris argues that New England should not
wince because Henry James, in his extended essay on Nathaniel
Hawthorne in 1879, had termed New England literature "provincial." Since good literature is always provincial, "it does seem to us
that the provinciality which gives us Hawthorne, Holmes, Whittier,
Howells, Harte, and Lowell ought to be as well worth nurturing

and cultivating as the exquisite culture which has given us (and the rest of the universe) Mr. James.''

"The Negro question" was a major issue with Harris from his Turnwold days on. Harris's boyhood impressions of plantation slavery had been largely positive ones since Turner had been an indulgent master and since many of his slaves had remained with him after the collapse of the Confederacy. But "even the bare suggestion of [slavery's] reëstablishment is unsavory," wrote Harris in 1877, no matter how romantic and peaceful one's memories of life in the Old South might be. The Negro problem that had developed after the war, Harris believed, was both economic and psychological. Would the black populace be able to find work and survive in the South? What would be the psychological effects on blacks and Southern whites of federal intervention on behalf of the Negro? Harris felt that using the Negro as a political football for Northern interests was harmful to both black and white attitudes in the South. Harris hoped that education of the Negro would provide the solution, but he realized that education was going to take time, patience, and money. Harris never entirely freed himself of a conviction that the white race would have to patronize the black, while keeping the races socially distinct, if the Negro were going to triumph over inherent ignorance and weakness.

Although Harris shared in the racial prejudices of his day, he affirmed the integrity of all individuals, whether black or white; and he could not countenance unjust or inhumane actions by any member of the human race. As Jerry Allen Herndon has accurately observed, Harris was a "progressive conservative" who supported the cause of the Negro when others did not; but he still acknowledged the desirability of a segregated society.[28] In time, Harris became one of the most sensitive interpreters of the Southern Negro; and it is fair to observe that he could not have done so had he not subordinated at least some of his own preconceptions and prejudices to the higher calling of the artist, and had he not instinctively recognized a strange similarity between the deprivations of his own past and those of the Negro.

While he was busy addressing the Negro question in his editorials and reviewing current books and magazines for the *Constitution,* Harris happened to read an article in *Lippincott's* for December 1877 entitled "Folklore of the Southern Negroes." Although Harris had made some passing allusions to Negro folklore in one or two of Remus's songs, this essay by William Owens, which included a transcribed story called "Buh Rabbit and the Tar Baby," released a flood of memories in Harris's mind. Old Harbert and George Terrell had told him scores of fables about the animals' shenanigans, but Harris apparently had not previously thought them interesting enough for magazine publication. With the discovery of Owens's article in a major periodical, however, he changed his mind; and he followed his earlier instinct to put his seasoned storyteller, Uncle Remus, back in a plantation setting, this time as an old-time narrator of Negro folk tales.

The first of the plantation fables, "The Story of Mr. Rabbit and Mr. Fox as Told by Uncle Remus," was published under the heading "Negro Folklore" in the *Constitution* on July 20, 1879; and it later became the initial tale in Harris's first Uncle Remus volume. Most of the more than one hundred and eighty Remus stories that were published in book collections during the next twenty-seven years used the narrative frame that Harris created in this initial sketch, in which the six- or seven-year-old son of Miss Sally and Master John, owners of a large plantation in Middle Georgia, is found sitting at the knee of old Uncle Remus and listening raptly to his tale of Mr. Rabbit's outwitting of either Mr. Fox or one of the other stronger animals. Harris cautiously waited four months for readers' responses before printing his second folk tale, one which related the first part of the tar-baby episode as Harris had interpreted it. Mr. Rabbit was now called Brer Rabbit, and to Harris's great astonishment "Uncle Remus" was suddenly on everyone's lips.

Harris was encouraged by the popular response to Brer Rabbit's escapades to contribute several more Remus fables to the *Constitution,* and he augmented these with a series of aphoristic "Plantation Proverbs" that gave Remus additional stature as a humorist and as an Old South wise-man. Other papers soon started reprinting Remus's lore, and hundreds of letters from all around the nation began to pour in. Folklorists such as the Amazon researcher H. H. Smith and J. W. Powell of the Smithsonian's Bureau of Ethnology were impressed by the tales; and other readers, both Northern and Southern, wondered if Harris had plans for publishing them in book form. Although Harris was gratified by the attention his kind of New South literature was receiving, he nevertheless did not feel that he had created, but only recreated, a legacy of the Old South. In an editorial for April 9, 1880, which in a revised version became part of the introduction to his first volume of tales,

Harris wrote that he sought in the Remus legends to "preserve in permanent shape those curious mementoes of a period that will no doubt be sadly misrepresented by historians of the future." He also wanted to record the dialect of the Old South plantation legends — a dialect that revealed "the really poetic imagination," the "quaint and rugged humor," and the sensitiveness of the Negro.

Early in 1880, D. Appleton and Company had agent James C. Derby stop in Atlanta to speak with Harris about preparing a collection of his Remus tales, songs, and aphoristic sayings which Appleton proposed to publish under the title "Uncle Remus's Folk-Lore." Since Derby later recalled that Harris was "a very agreeable and intelligent gentleman, although diffident in the extreme,"[29] it is quite possible that Harris, who continued to think of himself as only a cornfield journalist, would have confined his Remus sketches to the pages of the *Constitution* had Appleton's not taken the initiative. Harris's first book, which contained some legends and songs not previously printed, bore 1881 as its publication date; but it was actually released at the end of November 1880, in time for the Christmas gift-book trade.

Happily retitled *Uncle Remus: His Songs and His Sayings,* it included a full-lipped, stereotyped portrait of Remus by a Southern painter, J. H. Moser, who also did other Negro plates for the book, and animal drawings by Frederick S. Church of New York. As Cousins notes, Appleton's saw Harris's book as a marketable addition to their catalogue of humorous publications, and Moser and Church were retained to illustrate the "humor" of the book rather than its more sensitive tone as a study in animal and human traits.[30] Several years passed before Harris found an illustrator who evoked the spirit of Remus and the little boy as human companions and who were surrounded by the highly individualized members of the animal kingdom which Remus spun out of his imagination.[31]

Within four months, *Uncle Remus* had sold ten thousand copies and had been enthusiastically reviewed in hundreds of the nation's newspapers. Ironically, while Harris was working hard to leave his mark on Southern letters as an editor calling for a social and literary renaissance in his region, he inadvertently carved out an enduring literary reputation by serving as the "compiler," as he modestly called himself, of what he thought were only minor sketches of prewar Southern life and character. His sudden success made him feel so much more self-conscious for a time that he took a pencil and carefully revised some sixty-six pages of dialect in his personal copy of *Uncle Remus,* for he was afraid that he had not been accurate enough. When he contemplated a second Remus collection, he prepared ahead of time a plan for organizing the book; for he believed that a "literary" man had better put more "art" into his next volume. Another effect of Harris's new fame was that he could no longer hide his reticent personality behind his pen during the working day; interviewers began to ask for appointments; and Harris's red hair, freckles, and shy and self-deprecating manner were soon subjects for national, rather than merely regional, amusement. As Walter Hines Page observed, it was hard to believe, but true, that "Joe Harris does not appreciate Joel Chandler Harris."[32]

As the months passed, Harris became aware that his tales were the record of a folklore that was fast disappearing from public memory. He was eager to receive in letters, and occasionally orally, outlines and motifs from readers who remembered having heard Remus-type tales in their youth, or from Negroes who had lived in the Old South. First of all, these letters "verified," as Harris termed it, many of the stories he had already written. As late as 1905 he was still trying to maintain the standard that he had set for himself with the earliest Remus legends: to publish as dialect stories only those tales that he could vouch for as authentic Negro narratives. Second, contributions from readers either helped Harris recall additional stories or suggested new ones that he could put into old plantation dialect. However, it is an important corrective to Harris's disclaimer that he was only a "compiler" of the Remus tales to note that he often spun several-page tales from the one-paragraph summaries sent to him by his readers; and an unpublished letter to the folklorist Charles Colcock Jones written in March 1883 reveals that Harris was even willing to pay for outlines of stories from the Sea Islands and coastal plantations.[33]

But the point is that Harris did not originate the tales, or "cook" them up out of his imagination; rather, he allowed his discriminating ear and his feel for human psychology and behavior to give bare but authentic outlines life. If Uncle Remus had heard the stories that Harris's readers had sent him, he would have told them the way Harris wrote them; and in the telling lies the art.

CHAPTER 2

Man of Letters

I *The Major Period*

H ARRIS'S success with his first book led to several events in
1881 and 1882. Although his royalties were not substantial, he
could now afford to rent a larger house on Gordon Street in West
End for his growing family; and two years later he bought the place
and the five surrounding acres. In time, he added a series of rooms
to accommodate six growing children as well as good-hearted and
self-reliant Grandmother Harris, who had moved earlier from
Eatonton. In the 1890s, Harris's house became popularly known as
"The Sign of the Wren's Nest," so named by the family when
Harris refused to "break up a home" built by wrens in the mail-
box. Harris found that he enjoyed writing in the new house with his
children around him more than in the office, and he apparently felt
most secure and relaxed when he could work within the sound of
Essie's voice. He acquired the habit of riding one of the mule-
drawn trolleys to work in the morning, picking up his assignments
for the day, and then returning home to complete them. In the eve-
nings, he read, answered correspondence, and did his "own" writing — for he was now being asked for contributions by *Scribner's,
The Critic, Century, Harper's,* and other magazines. He habitually
apologized for his "literary" self, but he could no longer deny its
reality.

Harris felt extremely complimented when Mark Twain wrote him
an appreciative letter in the summer of 1881 and invited him to
Hartford. Twain also asked "Uncle Remus," as Harris was now
popularly known, whether he had found a Negro ghost story about
a golden arm among his Georgia tales. Harris, who wrote on

August 6 to thank Twain, insisted with his usual diffidence that his book had "no basis of literary art to stand upon" and that "the matter and not the manner has attracted public attention" in the North. No, he did not know the ghost story; but, if Twain could send him an outline or a manuscript, he would try to "verify it here."[1] In spite of his modest disclaimers, it is obvious that Harris's ambition was now being aroused; for he asked Twain in his letter how he should publish his Remus stories for his best economic advantage.

In Twain's response of August 10, which was candid and detailed, he told Harris that he was only deluding himself in thinking that the stories offered content but no art: "Uncle Remus is most deftly drawn, & is a lovable & delightful creation; he, & the little boy, & their relations with each other, are bright fine literature, & worthy to live, for their own sakes." The stories themselves "are only alligator pears [avocados] — one merely eats them for the sake of the salad-dressing."[2] As for the exigencies of publishing, Twain recommended that Harris contact James R. Osgood of Boston to explore the possibility of selling a second collection of Remus tales by subscription through traveling book agents, because the author's return was substantially higher this way. Also, Twain cordially told "Uncle Remus" to keep his name before the public, but "at the same time keep the public unsatisfied" by printing a story in the magazines once every three months or so. Harris had recently been averaging five sketches a month, and Twain counseled: "I wouldn't let them have such generous meals as you have been giving them. — For the ficklest people in the world are the public."

Twain's letter also contained a partially dialectical transcription of "De Woman wid de Gold'n Arm," the Negro ghost story that had proven to be one of his most successful platform readings. As did Harris in the Remus stories, Twain acknowledged the primacy of the oral folk tradition in explaining the origin of the old tale: he had heard it as a child sitting at the knee of Old Uncle Daniel, a black slave of Florida, Missouri. Twain thought Harris could more effectively than he put the story into full dialectical form: "Work up the atmosphere with your customary skill & it will 'go' in print." But Harris would not use the tale until he had first verified it. Within four months Harris had found a Georgia version of the tale, which he published as "A Ghost Story" in the *Century Magazine* for August 1883, and which he included in the collection *Nights*

with Uncle Remus later that year. With characteristic honesty
Harris included a note mentioning Twain's Missouri version.

Twain wrote Harris again in December 1881 to reiterate his
invitation to drop by Hartford and to vouch a second time for
James Osgood's professional expertise. In the spring of 1882,
Twain, who had another idea, arranged for his old friend Joseph
Twichell to visit Harris at the *Constitution* office to see if he would
be interested in accompanying Twain on a lecture tour. Harris
declined the offer because of the painful shyness that his success in
Atlanta had in no way alleviated; but Twain, who was nothing if
not persistent, wrote in April to invite Harris to meet him and
Osgood in New Orleans in early May. There Twain could talk to
him about "a device" that he thought would get around Harris's
stage fright, and Osgood could tell him how to chart his course in
the publishing world. Harris, who relented a little because of
Twain's persistence, met him and Osgood at their hotel the last
Sunday in April 1882. Later that morning, George Washington
Cable, who was also part of Twain's lecture-tour plans, dropped by
to take the men to the service at his Presbyterian church, and then
on a tour of the city.

If the socializing was intended to help Harris relax and make him
more receptive to Twain's suggestions, the scheme was only partially successful. When the group gathered in Cable's study on
Monday afternoon for a storytelling session with Cable's and his
sister Nettie's children, Harris refused to follow Twain's and
Cable's readings with some of his own Remus tales;[3] furthermore,
although he did agree to let Osgood publish his next two books, he
again declined the lecture-tour proposal. Twain was disappointed.
He had read the tar-baby story in public and found it to be
extremely popular,[4] and had hoped that his "device" of having
Cable and himself read first might show Uncle Remus that there
was nothing to worry about.

Twain shared his perception of Harris's nature a year later in
Chapter 47 of *Life on the Mississippi,* in which he dramatized only
slightly the May afternoon's events:

[Harris] was said to be very shy. He is a shy man. Of this there is no
doubt. It may not show on the surface, but the shyness is there. After days
of intimacy one wonders to see that it is still in about as strong force as
ever. There is a fine and beautiful nature hidden behind it, as all know who
have read the Uncle Remus book; and a fine genius, too, as all know by

the same sign. . . . He deeply disappointed a number of children who had flocked eagerly to Mr. Cable's house to get a glimpse of the illustrious sage and oracle of the nation's nurseries. They said: —

"Why, he's white!"

They were grieved about it. So, to console them, the book was brought, that they might hear Uncle Remus's Tar-Baby story from the lips of Uncle Remus himself — or what, in their outraged eyes, was left of him. But it turned out that he had never read aloud to people, and was too shy to venture the attempt now. Mr. Cable and I read from books of ours, to show him what an easy trick it was; but his immortal shyness was proof against even this sagacious strategy, so we had to read about Brer Rabbit ourselves.[5]

Harris eventually accepted Twain's earlier invitation to come north for a visit, stopping off in Hartford in the spring of 1883 while en route to see his Canadian in-laws. He had bypassed a chance to see Twain at his home the previous spring when Harris and his editor-in-chief, Evan Howell, had attended a dinner in honor of American writers and artists at the Tile Club in New York City. At the dinner he had again refused to read one of his tales, or even to speak informally, and he had skipped a second dinner invitation entirely, as well as an appointment with D. Appleton and Company, his first publisher, in his haste to get back to Atlanta and to the security of his family. Harris spoke later of his "awkwardness and embarrassment" at dinner parties,[6] and Twain wrote him in September 1882 that he had heard of his "admirable stupefaction" at the Tile Club.

Harris favorably reviewed in 1882 and 1885 two of Twain's works — *The Stolen White Elephant, Etc.,* and *Huckleberry Finn,*[7] — for the *Constitution,* and the relationship between the two writers formally closed with Twain's note of thanks for a birthday letter that Harris had published in *The Critic* in November 1885. Harris wrote in his open letter that Twain added "salt to youth and season to old age" and that there was no more wholesome work of fiction in America than *Huckleberry Finn:* "Here we behold human character stripped of all tiresome details; we see people growing and living; we laugh at their humor, share their griefs; and, in the midst of it all, behold we are taught the lesson of honesty, justice and mercy." When Twain wrote Harris in late November that he, too, believed in Huck — despite the "mud" that critics were flinging at him — he added, "it's a great refreshment to my faith to have a man back me up who has been where such boys live,

& knows what he is talking about.'' The two writers would not meet
again or correspond; but, to judge from their perceptive and enthusiastic comments about each other, and from their similar experiences as young journalists who grew up close to the folk traditions
of the Old South, Uncle Remus and Mark Twain were never really
out of communication.

While continuing to fulfill his editorial responsibilities for the
Constitution, Harris, motivated by his discussions with Twain and
Osgood, began regularly to publish his stories in book form. *Nights
with Uncle Remus,* released in November 1883 by Osgood and
again illustrated by Frederick Church, was an ambitious collection
of seventy folktales, as compared to only thirty-four in the first volume; additionally, Harris expanded his cast of characters to include
Aunt Tempy, Daddy Jack, and 'Tildy, the house girl, as foils to
Remus and as narrators in their own right. Again, Harris sought to
verify every story. While drawing on his own plantation recollections and the contributions of interested correspondents, Harris
had another enjoyable and fruitful experience gathering tales firsthand in the summer of 1882. He had been waiting for the Atlanta
train in the railroad station in Norcross, Georgia, some twenty
miles northeast of Atlanta in Gwinnett County, when he overheard
some Negro workers cracking jokes and telling stories. Soon Harris
laughed with them, becoming as relaxed and as unself-conscious
among these Negroes as he had been with the blacks on Turner's
plantation twenty years earlier. Then he himself told the tar-baby
legend ''by way of a feeler,'' followed by another tale after he saw
how much the group had enjoyed the first one. For almost two
hours, Harris recalled, the Negroes vied with each other to see who
could tell the best stories; and Harris carried home as many of these
examples of the oral tradition at work as he could remember in
order to compare them with notes and other stories he had already
gathered. A rare moment of relaxation had borne a rich harvest.

Harris's thirty-one-page footnoted introduction to *Nights with
Uncle Remus* reveals how much reading he had done in folklore
commentaries and collections since publishing *Uncle Remus.*
Surveying the Amazon studies of Charles F. Hartt, Theal's *Kaffir
Folk-lore,* W. H. I. Bleek's *Hottentot Fables,* and the work of
J. W. Powell of the Smithsonian and other researchers, Harris discusses the considerable parallels between the folklore of the Southern Negroes and that of African, South American, and Indian
tribes. Finally, however, he seems unsure whether the apparent uni-

versality of the animal legends means that the tales arose spontaneously, or whether the intriguing similarities among so many of the tales argues for cultural cross-fertilization. The response to Harris's second book was as overwhelmingly favorable and enthusiastic as it had been to the first one. However, nine years passed before Harris had gathered and verified a sufficient number of plantation fables to justify a third Remus volume.

An ironic sidelight to Harris's attempt to ensure the authenticity of his own plantation stories was the humorous public skirmish called the ''Banjo Controversy'' that occurred when Harris published an article on ''Plantation Music'' in *The Critic* for December 15, 1883. Harris wrote that he had never seen a Negro play a banjo on the plantation; rather, the usual instruments were the quills (Pan's pipes), the fiddle, and the fife and flute. Readers immediately wrote to *The Critic* and to other magazines and newspapers to cite locales where they had seen the banjo played and to claim that Harris was mistaken. *The Critic* for June 28, 1884, the *New York Tribune,* and other papers carried George Washington Cable's statement that he had heard the banjo played in New Orleans but that the fiddle was a hundred times more common. It was possible, Cable thought, that Harris had never seen a Negro with a banjo. In a letter to Harris a month later, Cable agreed that the fiddle was the favorite plantation instrument; with that the ''controversy'' was over.[8]

In the 1880s Harris followed Twain's advice and regularly wrote stories for the magazines. During this period, Harris's editorial work for the *Constitution* helped to broaden his literary vision of Southern life and society and to include in his fiction more than just the ''quarters'' on the old plantation. When the first International Cotton Exposition was held in Atlanta from October through December 1881, Grady, Harris, and other journalists in the South, as well as the North, recognized that a new industrialized South could be a stimulus to national growth and postwar unity. Harris was obviously thinking about the problems of disorientation and reconciliation, the effects of the Civil War on middle- and lower-class whites and on the Negro, and Southern economic and social patterning in general when he composed a series of magazine stories from 1882–84.

In *The Romance of Rockville* (1878), Harris had made his first examination of the Southern social strata, but he now resumed his investigation of Southern life with renewed energy. In the fall of

1882 James Osgood had responded enthusiastically to a draft of
"Mingo," a sensitive postwar study of class resentment and mis-
understanding in the South, and he urged Harris to continue contributions in this vein. That spring Harris published in *Century*
magazine a vivid novelette about North Georgia mountaineers and
moonshiners, *At Teague Poteet's*. Osgood's firm published *Mingo
and Other Sketches* in 1884, a collection of these two stories plus
two others with more broadly developed plantation settings than
were contained in the Remus tales. The public was surprised and
impressed to see this new facet of Joel Chandler Harris's art, and
his local-color stories were very favorably reviewed. As with the
Remus tales, Harris's own deprived background as a Georgia
Cracker led him to identify strongly with the blacks and poor
whites he portrayed.

By the end of 1886, the names of both of the *Constitution's* associate editors had become household words. Henry Grady's finest
hour came on December 22, 1886, when he gave his address "The
New South" before a banquet meeting of the New England Society
that was held at Delmonico's in New York City. Among the 360
persons attending the banquet were many of America's most successful businessmen and financiers: Seth Thomas, H. M. Flagler,
John H. Inman, J. Pierpont Morgan, Russell Sage, and others.
After a toast by General W. T. Sherman, Grady began talking of
the promise that the South, reunited with the North, held for
America. He used as his text a quotation from Benjamin H. Hill:
"There was a South of slavery and secession — that South is dead.
There is a South of union and freedom — that South, thank God, is
living, breathing, growing every hour." Very quickly Grady's
cadences, his humor, and his images of the defeated Confederate
soldier's return to a devastated landscape and his subsequent hard
work to build a new life, a new society, and a solvent economy
began to bring his audience to their feet with cheers and applause.
Grady added with marvelous effect that the New South took no
time to apologize or be sullen about the past, or even to fault General Sherman — "though some people think he is a kind of careless
man about fire." Instead, the New South had gone to work, and
she was "thrilling with the consciousness of growing power and
prosperity." The South extended its hand to the North in comrade-
ship and brotherhood, to help all citizens achieve their "common
glory as Americans."[9]

Grady's major purpose in going to New York was to attract

industrial interests to the South; and, although his precise effect on the Southern economy cannot be measured, he was suddenly thrown into the national limelight as the "great pacificator." Unfortunately, Grady died only three years after making his famous speech, but his optimism and vision endured in the area he had named "the New South." Harris and others on the *Constitution*'s staff published a memorial volume about Grady in 1890, to which Harris contributed a sixty-page biographical sketch. What especially impressed Harris was Grady's selflessness. In serving the larger cause of rebuilding the South, Grady had consistently declined to enhance his own image by seeking public office — even when he had been petitioned by Atlanta's leading citizens to do so. He saw early in his career that journalism was his forte, and through his profession and his natural abilities as an orator he helped the South rise phoenixlike out of the ashes of war to find a new life beyond sectionalism and beyond despair.[10]

By the mid-1880s, Harris's name had also grown so familiar that the Chicago humorist Eugene Field was moved in late 1885 or early 1886 to spoof him by circulating bogus biographical sketches in the national press. Field, who wrote that Harris was the son of missionary parents in Joel, Africa, and that he had been named after his birthplace, stated that he had come to America and had served valorously in the Civil War but that his grief over the loss of his sweetheart during the engagement had turned his hair completely white. Love had again entered his life, however, and Harris was soon to wed the niece of Stonewall Jackson. Harris's success as a writer, Field added in a later supplement, had made him worth two million dollars, which he used to help the needy. Harris grinned at this latest instance of personal journalism, for he had long participated in the tradition himself. In an interview with a *Constitution* reporter in August, Harris announced that he was soon departing for Chicago; when asked "What for?" he calmly responded, "To kill Eugene Field."

So many readers took Field's account as true, however, that Harris agreed to publish a brief corrective biography in *Lippincott's* for April 1886. In "An Accidental Author," Harris claimed that his career as a writer began somewhat accidentally. Yet his precise use of dialect, his careful plans for the second Remus volume, and his numerous revisions of his local-color stories, especially,[11] argue that Harris was guilty of false modesty when he closed his essay with the following disclaimer: "I . . . know nothing at all of what is termed literary art. I have had no opportunity to nourish any serious literary ambition, and the possibility is that if such an opportunity had presented itself I would have refused to take advantage of it.''

As the decade progressed, magazine editors were certainly doing their best to put more "opportunities" in Harris's way. Thanks to the encouragement and editorial assistance of Richard Watson Gilder, Harris authored five local-color stories for *Scribner's* and *Century*, and these were subsequently collected in *Free Joe and Other Georgian Sketches* (1887), published by Charles Scribner's Sons.[12] The most poignant of these tales about separation and reconciliation, and probably Harris's most accomplished short story, was "Free Joe and the Rest of the World" (1884).

A fortuitous result of Harris's magazine work during this period was his introduction to the drawings of Arthur Burdett Frost, who had contributed four sensitive illustrations to "Free Joe" in *Century*. In 1886 Frost's editors had sent him to meet with Harris for a tour of the Georgia highlands in search of "types" for forthcoming illustrations, and the two men spent a day in the Marietta area. The two artists found themselves to be kindred spirits: they not only looked alike (both had red hair and were similar in build), but they tended to be apologetic and diffident about their own work. However, each man was most enthusiastic about the other's art, and a warm relationship developed that would continue, in their correspondence, until 1904. With the third Uncle Remus volume in 1892, Frost became Harris's favorite illustrator.[13]

By the later 1880s, Harris's place as America's most accomplished dialect writer and portrayer of the Negro was assured. Thomas Nelson Page's dialect stories about the old regime focused on sentimental and romantic episodes in the lives of Virginia aristocrats and their loyal slaves; but, popular as Page was, critics of the day saw Harris as the more authentic artist. Harris was made a charter member of the American Folklore Society when it was founded in the late 1880s. He felt, however, that the credit for bringing Negro dialect and character into literature was properly due to Mississippi's Irwin Russell whose poem "Christmas Night in the Quarters," published in 1876, was, Harris believed, the first important Negro dialect writing in America. Unfortunately, Russell's career was cut short by alcoholism, and he died in 1879 at the age of twenty-six.[14] Harris was highly complimentary of Russell in his introduction to a collection of his poems in 1888.

Fatigue and a series of minor illnesses slowed Harris's work between 1884 and 1889, but relaxation with his family and enjoyable hours in his extensive rose gardens began to rejuvenate him. Perhaps this strong dose of home-life caused Harris to write his first volume of stories in which children play major roles, *Daddy Jake, the Runaway, and Short Stories Told After Dark* (1889).[15] The stories in this collection concern the adventures of Lucien and Lillian (named after two of Harris's own offspring) and their favorite plantation friend, Daddy Jake, who had run away after cruel treatment by an overseer. The Daddy Jake episode ends happily, and thirteen additional Uncle Remus tales round off the book. Readers of all ages liked *Daddy Jake,* and eight editions had already been ordered from the Century Company before its official release. Harris shifted back to adult fiction in 1891 with *Balaam and His Master and Other Sketches and Stories,*[16] six tales about slaves and masters and about the economic and social disruption caused by the Civil War.

The 1890s proved to be Harris's most productive decade. Twelve more books and a new edition of an earlier one followed *Balaam,* and Harris tried all the while to maintain his normal workload at the *Constitution.* There were, of course, setbacks, both psychological and physiological. Seven-year-old Linton died of diphtheria in 1890, and the next year saw the death of sturdy Grandmother Harris, who had maintained her spirits and that of the family's despite a lingering illness. Additionally, Harris's own physical and mental health fluctuated periodically, and he realized by 1900 that retirement from the "newspaper grind," as he had begun to call it, might be the only way to stabilize his condition for awhile, at least, and to provide him an opportunity for the literary work that was proving to be more and more congenial.

Some of the books Harris wrote during the decade were done easily and instinctively. Harris's autobiographical narrative *On the Plantation* appeared in 1892,[17] as did a third Uncle Remus volume, *Uncle Remus and His Friends,*[18] which seemed to mark the end of Harris's work with his veteran storyteller and plantation sage. In this book the "little boy" is older, more independent, and more skeptical about Remus's imaginative recreation of the "creetur" kingdom. As if to confirm what the stories themselves implied, Harris announced that this book would be Remus's last appearance; he would no longer bother the public with his "fantasies," however worthwhile the "unadulterated human nature" in the stories might be. However, Harris's announcement about Remus's demise was premature, for the public was so taken with the fourth volume that it demanded a fifth — Harris in time provided it.

Harris revealed the considerable diversity of his interests as a man of letters in helping Essie translate a collection of French folk tales by Frederic Ortoli that was published as *Evening Tales* in 1893[19] and in writing a brisk but right-wing, chauvinistic narrative history of Georgia for high-school students in 1896.[20] Harris also found time between *Constitution* assignments to cover the disastrous Sea Islands hurricane for *Scribner's* in the fall of 1893, but much of his leisure and creative energy was directed toward the world of children. Harris wrote a series of five volumes of fanciful adventures for young readers before the end of the decade, and one more to complete the collection in 1903: *Little Mr. Thimblefinger* (1894), *The Story of Aaron* (1895), *Mr. Rabbit at Home* (1895), *Aaron in the Wildwoods* (1897), *Plantation Pageants* (1899), and *Wally Wanderoon and His Story-Telling Machine* (1903).[21]

In 1895 Appleton's issued a new edition of *Uncle Remus: His Songs and His Sayings,* with illustrations by Frost. Harris had always encouraged Frost to interpret Remus and the creatures in his own way, and the illustrator's notebooks for the 1890s are especially replete with rabbit-studies in various clothing and poses. The drawings that accompany the 1895 edition perfectly captured what Harris (and most of his readers, too, to judge from the reviews) thought Remus and the animals should look and act like. Harris dedicated the edition to Frost, and, praising his sensitivity, stated simply: "The book was mine, but now you have made it yours, both sap and pith." Although Harris admired Frost's work, he was unsure about the advisability of printing a new edition of *Uncle Remus* in 1895; almost in confirmation of Remus's continuing vitality and universal appeal, however, later that year he received a complimentary letter from Rudyard Kipling. Harris had just reviewed *The Jungle Book* favorably in the *Book-Buyer;* and, after thanking him for the notice, Kipling wrote:

I wonder if you could realize how "Uncle Remus," his sayings, and the sayings of the noble beasties ran like wild fire through an English public school when I was about fifteen. We used to go to battle (with boots and bolsters and such-like) against those whom we did not love, to the tune of *Ty-yi-tungalee; I eat um pea, I pick um pea,* etc., and I remember the bodily bearing into a furze-bush of a young fag solely because his nick-

name had been "Rabbit" before the tales invaded the school and — well, we assumed that he ought to have been "bawn an' bred in a briar-patch," and gorse was the most efficient substitute. And six years ago in India, meeting an old schoolmate of those days, we found ourselves quoting whole pages of "Uncle Remus" that had got mixed in with the fabric of the old school life.[22]

In the 1890s Harris also tried his hand again at novel-writing. Since composing local-color stories for the magazines had given him confidence in handling character and theme across a broad social setting, Harris returned with a surer pen to some motifs and figures that he had first treated in *The Romance of Rockville* (1878). Despite his apologies for the "gaps and lapses" in his book,[23] *Sister Jane: Her Friends and Acquaintances* (1896) is a more significant novel than Harris and some of his critics have realized because it is a psychologically complex portrait of the author himself. Harris clearly identifies with his diffident and self-effacing narrator, and he projects his own history into the story's theme of illegitimate birth and its consequences.

Harris's next volume, *Tales of the Home Folks in Peace and War* (1898),[24] included stories that had appeared in *Scribner's, Atlantic Monthly,* and other journals. The majority of these tales feature the Middle Georgia scene during and after the Civil War, and they also develop some of Harris's favorite public themes: reconciliation, courage, the rewards of love and the price of hatred, and the economic aftermath of the war. But two of the stories which are of a different nature deserve attention because they reflect Harris's personal attitudes and beliefs in the latter 1890s. "The Late Mr. Watkins of Georgia: His Relation to Oriental Folk-Lore" is a tongue-in-cheek burlesque on the "science" of comparative folklore. A postmortem of sorts on Harris's work with the Remus tales, it reveals his skepticism about the ability of folklorists to prove how, or even whether, tales can be transmitted from one culture to another. Although Harris would publish additional Remus legends during 1903–1905, he did so reluctantly; he had used up most of his verified material and had grown impatient with the Remus–little boy frame. Moreover, the signs are that by the mid-1890s his public responsibility as the South's resident "folklorist" had become something of an embarrassment. The professional folklorists, Harris realized, to say nothing of amateurs like himself, could draw few verifiable conclusions with their so-called science. As he states in his preface to *Uncle Remus and His Friends,* "at the end of

investigation and discussion Speculation stands grinning''[25] in comparative folklore. In *Wally Wanderoon and His Story-Telling Machine* (1903) Harris again burlesqued the study of folklore; and he suggested that the real values in a well-told story lay not in any scientific content but in the humanity and moral themes it portrayed.

The other story from *Tales of the Home Folks* that reveals Harris's personal attitudes in the 1890s more indirectly, "A Belle of St. Valerien," is a semiautobiographical tale set in Esther LaRose's Quebec. Although a beautiful young Catholic girl and a priest are the strongest characters in the tale, the depiction of Euphrasie Charette's American suitor as an uncouth and even repulsive figure reflects Harris's continuing negative self-image despite his popular success. It is significant that Harris's favorable portrait of Canadian Catholic society was written shortly after his letters began to show his increasing interest in Catholicism. In a letter in 1896, Harris spoke of "the prejudices and doubts and fictions" that Protestantism had "educated" into him, and he indicated that Catholicism was growing more attractive to him every day.[26] In his insecurity, Harris was drawn by the ritual structure and confessional emphasis of the Mother Church. John Henry Newman had become one of his favorite writers, furthermore, and he liked to loan his copy of the *Apologia* to his friends.

As the decade drew to a close, Harris was growing increasingly impatient with the newspaper routine. Although the fluctuations in his health contributed to his restlessness, his sense of freedom and the personal satisfaction, and, indeed, personal therapy, that his own writing was giving him brought him to the verge of resigning from the *Constitution*. A letter to his teen-age daughters in the spring of 1898 is especially revealing, for Harris acknowledges in it the struggle that had been going on between his two selves, the journalist and the author:

As for myself — though you could hardly call me a real, sure enough author — I have anything but the vaguest ideas of what I am going to write; but when I take my pen in my hand, the rust clears away and the "other fellow" takes charge.... Now, I'll admit that I write the editorials for the paper. The "other fellow" has nothing to do with them, and, so far as I am able to get his views on the subject, he regards them with scorn and contempt; though there are rare occasions when he helps me out on a Sunday editorial. He is a creature hard to understand, but, so far as I can understand him, he's a very sour, surly fellow until I give him an oppor-

tunity to guide my pen in subjects congenial to him; whereas, I am, as you know, jolly, good-natured, and entirely harmless.

Now, my "other fellow," I am convinced, would do some damage if I didn't give him an opportunity to work off his energy in the way he delights. I say to him, "Now, here's an editor who says he will pay well for a short story. He wants it at once." Then I forget all about the matter, and go on writing editorials and taking Celery Compound and presently my "other fellow" says sourly: "What about that story?" Then when night comes, I take up my pen, surrendering unconditionally to my "other fellow," and out comes the story, and if it is a good story I am as much surprised as the people who read it.[27]

Jay Martin feels that Harris's constitutional shyness, his avoidance of public appearances, and even his refusal to change his style of dress as he became older are all characteristics of "the psychic complex that underlies stuttering."[28] The split between Harris's vocational and avocational self, in other words, was part of a deeper psychological rift — in fact, as I have suggested, one that had developed in his childhood. Harris's deep-seated insecurity about his own identity and ability never left him; but, as he gave a freer and freer hand to the "other fellow" and deemphasized his journalistic self, he felt happier and found a more authentic style of life and work. His youthful impulse to become an accomplished creative writer was apparently the healthiest one, psychologically, all along.

As if in confirmation of his new openness with his other self, Harris created a character even more vital and engaging than Remus in *The Chronicles of Aunt Minervy Ann* (1899).[29] Aunt Minervy, a black woman living in Middle Georgia during Reconstruction, displays integrity, courage, and a canniness about human nature that are equaled only by her energy and aggressiveness. Harris was writing more boldly and assertively now, although with the same dialectical care that he had always taken. In 1898, he wrote to his editor at *Scribner's*, where the eight Minervy stories were first published, that he was "intensely absorbed in the series, more so than in anything I have ever written."[30]

During the same period of creative energy that produced Minervy Ann, Harris also discovered, and endeared to his public, his alter ego and spokesman on all subjects sacred and profane, Billy Sanders. Sanders began his literary career as a private in the Confederate Army in a *Saturday Evening Post* serial for June 1900, that was titled "The Kidnapping of President Lincoln." In this

humorous adventure tale, which proved very popular with the
Post's readers, Sanders's geniality, democracy, common sense, and
down-home Middle Georgia humor and prowess as a storyteller are
delightfully and realistically displayed. The Lincoln story and four
other Civil War tales were published by Doubleday as *On the Wing
of Occasions* in 1900,[31] and shortly afterwards Harris began to
include Billy Sanders in other tales and to use this "philosopher of
Shady Dale," as Harris tagged him, as an editorial spokesman and
rural sage in magazine essays.

Along with Harris's burst of creative activity came his decision to
retire, finally, from the *Constitution*. He had received an offer
from the *Century* editors fifteen years earlier to write regularly for
them in place of doing daily newspaper work; he had rejected that
proposition because its $2,500 yearly contract was inadequate to
support his growing family. But in the intervening years Harris,
learning from Twain's example, had begun to realize modest
returns from the books that the "other fellow" wrote; and, in the
summer of 1900 when McClure Phillips and Doubleday Page both
made him offers, Harris felt that the moment was right for a decision. He submitted his resignation to the *Constitution* on September 5, 1900, and he soon had signed a contract to write books at his
own pace for McClure. Although Harris averaged a book a year for
McClure, he still kept his stories and editorial essays, many of these
in Billy Sanders's voice, circulating among the magazines; and he
also sent occasional items to the *Constitution*. Most importantly,
he had at last earned the right to be the "other fellow" whenever he
chose.

II *Later Years*

Harris's new freedom from routine restored at least temporarily
his jaded sensibilities. He enjoyed leisurely hours in the parlor with
Essie and the children and warm afternoons bird-watching and
tending flowers and vegetables in his gardens on "Snap-Bean
Farm" — the acreage adjoining the house that Harris had playfully
named after Eugene Field's Sabine Farm. As Don Marquis recalls,
Harris was an excellent naturalist who enjoyed botany and orni-
thology and who saw a true organic relationship among all living
things.[32] Harris's love of the eternal order of nature may account in
part for his skepticism about man's more ephemeral creations. He
was always suspicious of anything new, Essie remembers, including

new furniture, new carpets, and new inventions. When electricity came to Atlanta, he had electric light fixtures temporarily attached to his gas chandeliers because such fixtures could be easily removed when the electricity "fad" had passed. Nevertheless, he did buy a typewriter and had even begun to compose at it by 1901 or so.

His last eight years turned out to be almost as productive as the 1890s. In 1900–1902, he contributed a series of Billy Sanders essays to a new magazine, *The World's Work,* and wrote four short stories for the *Saturday Evening Post* that were published in 1902 as *The Making of a Statesman, and Other Stories.*[33] During the same period Harris also began two novels that were motivated by his own continuing interest in the genre, by the popularity of the novel form in America generally, and by a proposition from William Dean Howells. In the spring of 1900, Howells had invited several English and American authors to write serialized novels for a newspaper syndicate that he was trying to organize. In June 1900 Harris wrote him that he had two books in mind that might suit his plan: "One Mile to Shady Dale," a novel about Georgia at the beginning of the Civil War, and "Qua," a Revolutionary War tale based on the actual adventures of an African prince in America.

Near the close of his letter, Harris observed with predictable modesty: "You know, of course, that so far as literary art is concerned, I am poverty-stricken; and you know, too, that my style and methods will cause you to pull your hair. You knew all about that before you invited me into the scheme."[34] Harris, who hoped to have the manuscripts to Howells by December, went to work that summer or fall on "Qua: A Romance of the Revolution." As Harris wrote the first seven chapters of his novel, he drew upon the historical materials he had gathered in the middle 1890s when preparing his *Stories of Georgia* textbook; and a brief reference to the character Qua also appears in *The Chronicles of Aunt Minervy Ann* (1899). Nonetheless, the book was never completed, perhaps because Harris stopped writing when he heard that Howells had abandoned his newspaper plan, or, as Thomas English suggests in his careful study of the "Qua" manuscript, because he felt unsure of his ability to sustain a narrative that was based on characters and events so remote from his own experiences and observations.[35]

"One Mile to Shady Dale" did materialize, however; it was reconceived as a postwar novel and published as *Gabriel Tolliver: A Story of Reconstruction* (1902)[36] after it had appeared as a serial in *The Era.* Once again, images and tensions from Harris's own life pervade the book, and their presence indicates that his search for himself continued unabated into his final years. The book is rambling and episodic, but contemporaneous and modern critics alike have generally found it to be the most balanced Reconstruction novel that the South produced. It has been called superior to Thomas Nelson Page's *Red Rock, A Chronicle of Reconstruction* (1898), which romanticizes the Old South, Cable's *John March, Southerner* (1894), which proselytizes too noticeably for social and political reform; and Thomas Dixon's *The Leopard's Spots* (1902) and *The Clansman* (1905), which are biased strongly toward the right.

Harris dedicated his novel to James Whitcomb Riley, who by 1902 had become a fast friend of the household. "Uncle Jeems," as the children called him, had been an avid reader of "Uncle Remus" since 1881; and the two men had exchanged letters and presentation volumes of their writings. In the spring of 1900 Riley had spent two weeks at the "Wren's Nest," and in 1902 they met each other at Lithia Springs, near Atlanta, for another fortnight of anecdote-swapping and companionship. Harris's relationship with Riley was probably the major friendship of his life, and it is unfortunate that so few materials exist for documenting it. Harris once recalled to an interviewer that the two weeks he spent with Uncle Jeems at Lithia Springs were the happiest he had ever known.[37]

Harris's health took another downward turn in the spring of 1902, when complications from a tooth infection and other disorders weakened him. But, cheered by receiving (upon his own insistence, in absentia) an honorary Doctorate of Literature from Emory College that June, he kept as busy as he could at his typewriter. He published the *Wally Wanderoon* volume in 1903 as well as a serialized Civil War novel, *A Little Union Scout,* in 1904.[38] During this period, Harris also experimented with versifying some Uncle Remus materials that he was apparently still gathering; and these echo the rhythms of plantation work songs and hymns that he had heard as a boy. The *Post* and *Century* published several of the story-songs, and Appleton collected them as *The Tar-Baby and Other Rhymes of Uncle Remus* in 1904.[39]

During 1903–1905 Harris put most of his remaining Remus legends into publishable form in *Metropolitan Magazine* and in *Collier's,* and he gathered these and other tales in *Told by Uncle Remus: New Stories of the Old Plantation* (1905).[40] Since more than twelve years had passed since Harris had done any serious work with Remus stories, this last major collection was both a personal housecleaning and an epilogue to the entire Remus tradition and the pastoral plantation days. While placing his old-time Negro in final perspective, Harris was also taking a last look at the role, image, and expectations of the black man at the beginning of the new century. As Arlin Turner has indicated, state laws on voting qualifications and segregation that had been passed in the 1890s made some Southerners (including Booker T. Washington) breathe easier; for the question of public rights for the Negro could now be postponed for the moment.[41]

Harris, too, was glad to beg the thorny question of civil equality, and he considered in three articles written for the *Saturday Evening Post* in early 1904 other aspects of "the Negro problem."[42] In "The Negro as the South Sees Him," Harris corrected some misconceptions about the antebellum Negro by pointing out that the black "mammy," the field hand, and the family retainer of the old days were more often than not practical, hard-working, outspoken, and humble in the right sense — that is, not servile. Harris found it ironical that Stowe's *Uncle Tom's Cabin,* while it taught "that the possibilities of slavery anywhere and everywhere are shocking to the imagination," also revealed some of the more romantic aspects of slavery. Her cruelest character, Harris reminded the reader, was not a Southerner but a Northerner, Simon Legree.

"The Negro of To-Day" and "The Negro Problem" returned to themes that Harris had frequently addressed in the 1870s and 1880s. For Harris, the "problem" of the Negro was an elusive one that may have been the result of several overlapping movements and attitudes. Many liked to talk of it as a crisis of "social equality," but this term was difficult to handle satisfactorily, Harris rationalized, because there is no such thing as mental, physical, or social equality between any two members of the human race. Harris agreed that Northern politicians spawned injustice in the South and that the Negro was manipulated and exploited as a consequence. By 1904, Harris had somewhat tempered, however, his view that blacks had to be patronized by the whites if they were to succeed in America. The Negro needed to be free to demonstrate thrift, industry, and responsibility. The tremendous increase in black ownership of property and business was encouraging, he continued, as were the advances that education was bringing to the Negro. Harris concluded with the observation that the Negro had to solve the problem that all men had to solve: "the problem of moral, social and industrial development." The only solution, for every man, was "hard work and right living."

Harris's last years saw no relaxation of his nervousness about public appearances. He had not been willing to travel to Oxford, Georgia, to receive his honorary degree from Emory College; and he had declined an invitation to visit his home town of Eatonton for a celebration in his honor. Early in 1905 he turned down the University of Pennsylvania's offer of another honorary degree, which it would award only if he could be present to receive it. Fortunately, no personal appearance was required when Harris was elected in May to membership in the newly formed American Academy of Arts and Letters. The two Jameses, Howells, Twain, and Thomas Bailey Aldrich were among those chosen; and it is a telling index of Harris's national esteem at the close of his life that he was the only Southern writer selected for admission.

The severest test of Harris's constitutional reclusiveness came in 1905, but the results could not have been happier. On October 20, President and Mrs. Theodore Roosevelt were to visit Atlanta where Roosevelt was to make an address at the Georgia State Fair and speak at a luncheon afterwards; Mrs. Roosevelt insisted that she wanted to meet "Uncle Remus" while they were in the city. The Roosevelts had long admired Harris's work, and Teddy had sent him warm and complimentary letters in 1901 and 1902. Harris's former boss, Clark Howell of the *Constitution,* took care of the arrangements. Reputedly, he appointed several friends to escort Harris to the train station; and he instructed them to " 'see that he's there if you have to hog-tie him.' " Harris shook hands with the President and his wife at the station but then quickly disappeared into the crowd while the band was playing "Hail to the Chief."[43] However, Mrs. Roosevelt got revenge by making sure that Harris was standing with her later that day on a balcony overlooking Peachtree Street to review the parade.

The culmination of the day's events for Harris, and probably the most memorable moment in his life, was at the Presidential banquet when Roosevelt turned to him and announced that he was going to ill repay the hospitality he had received by causing for a moment or two " 'acute discomfort to a man of whom I am very fond — Uncle Remus.' " Roosevelt then said:

Presidents may come and presidents may go, but Uncle Remus stays put. Georgia has done a great many things for the Union, but she has never done more than when she gave Mr. Joel Chandler Harris to American literature.... Where Mr. Harris seems to me to have done one of his greatest services is that he has written what exalts the South in the mind of every man who reads it, and yet what has not even a flavor of bitterness toward any other part of the Union.[44]

Roosevelt struck a major chord in Harris's work in praising its non-sectional perspectives, and the two men also found that they shared other viewpoints and attitudes. Two and a half years later, in November 1907, Roosevelt and the First Lady invited Harris to visit them at the White House; and Uncle Remus accepted. At his own insistence, Harris was accompanied to provide moral support by his son Julian and by his new friend Don Marquis; but, as it turned out, Harris needed no bolstering this time. According to Roosevelt's own account of the evening, after half an hour Harris "was talking and laughing freely, and exchanging anecdotes and criticisms, and comparing reminiscences.... We felt that our gentle-natured, sweet-tempered, almost humble-minded guest was also a really great man, a man utterly fearless in his flaming anger against wrong and oppression."[45]

Roosevelt's is one of only three or four accounts that attest to Harris's ability to relax with a small group of friends; when the setting was just right, Harris could lower his defenses. As Billy Sanders later summed up the visit to Washington, "Well, I came away from the White House might'ly hope up, feelin' that Teddy is the President of the whole country, an' not of a party. I felt jest like I had been on a visit to some friend that I had n't seed in years. An' I went back to the hotel an' snored as loud as ef I'd 'a' been on my own shuck mattress, an' dreamed that the men in Wall Street had promised to be reasonably honest atter the first of Jinawary."[46]

Although *Told by Uncle Remus* (1905) was the last volume that Harris had contracted to publish through McClure, he was not yet ready to push his typewriter to the back of the desk. In fact, he turned in 1906-1907 to a major new enterprise that would draw on his talents as both author and editor. Harris's son Julian had succeeded in raising enough money from financial backers to inaugurate a new Southern literary periodical and had persuaded Harris to be its editor. Harris had been reluctant at first; but, when Julian's corporation agreed that Harris could have complete authority over the journal's content and even its advertising, he agreed to the offer. Despite his retirement, Harris was continuing to attract national attention, and visits at the "Wren's Nest" by major fig-

ures like Andrew Carnegie and Samuel Gompers probably reinforced his decision to enter actively into journalism again.

In one sense, *Uncle Remus's Magazine,* or *The Optimist* as
Harris almost decided to call it, was the kind of periodical that
Joseph Addison Turner's protégé Joe Harris had always wanted to
publish. Its motto was "Typical of the South — National in
Scope," and in his editorial for the first number of June 1907,
Harris again sounded the call that had been echoing through his
books and essays for over thirty years: all Americans are neighbors
and can find mutual benefit in transcending sectional differences.
While Harris invited contributions from all his "neighbors," he
would have been less than honest had he not stated that the magazine would "encourage" the "cultivation of the rich field of poetry
and romance which, in the Southern States, offers a constant
invitation to those who aspire to deal in fictive literature."

The new Atlanta author Don Marquis was the associate editor;
but Harris normally did all the lead articles and book reviews. It is
characteristic of Harris's self-effacing behavior that when he wrote
book reviews he tried to disguise himself, even from his own staff,
as "Anne Macfarland," a genial, middle-aged Englishwoman.
Apparently Harris did not want to give the impression that the
whole magazine was just his own pet project. The staff members
were not fooled by his ruse, but they did not destroy the boss's illu-
sion. Harris's reviews of contemporary novelists emphasized the
need for optimistic studies in human nature in place of the sordid
portraits that the naturalistic writers drew. For example, he con-
demned the degenerate "buzzards" that people Edith Wharton's
House of Mirth, but E. W. Howe's *The Story of a Country Town*
left a vivid and lasting impression despite its grimness. On a different tack, Harris agreed that Henry James's *Portrait of a Lady* was
a fine book; he only wished that his diction were less "painful."

Through spokesman Billy Sanders, Harris had opportunity to
range over virtually any topic he chose. Billy often spoke against
mob rule, violence, dishonesty in politics, and prejudice; but, in a
variation of a technique that Harris had first used with his Atlanta
Remus, the "boys" on the *Uncle Remus* staff sometimes refused to
follow Sanders's advice. Cousins notes the irony of the fact that the
magazine declined to turn its editorial attention to muckraking, as
Sanders had once counseled; for, had it done so, the journal might
have realized wider circulation than it did.[47] However, Harris
wanted to avoid sensationalism, for he regarded the magazine as an

organ of optimism and reconciliation in the turbulent days of the early twentieth century. Sanders also played such a role in a novel for young people that Harris published in five installments in *Uncle Remus's Magazine* when he reconciles differences among characters in Shady Dale; but his Middle Georgia sense of humor is entertaining in its own right. *The Bishop and the Boogerman* was published in book form posthumously.[48]

In 1907, Frederick Stokes published an edition of six stories and five rhymes of Uncle Remus that was accompanied by multicolored cartoon illustrations done by J. M. Condé, who had contributed some of the drawings for *Told by Uncle Remus*. *Uncle Remus and Brer Rabbit*[49] is more a footnote to the Remus tradition than a significant addition, but the animal cartoons anticipate the comic strips and the movie cartoons that soon took a permanent place in American popular culture.

Harris's last work was another Civil War novel serialized in the *Saturday Evening Post* in late 1907. *The Shadow Between His Shoulder-Blades*[50] is again narrated by Billy Sanders, whose humorous and anecdotal recollections of his inconsequential role in the Civil War give the story a realistic texture and a naturalness that a more self-conscious attempt at adventure-building might have destroyed. We would like to think that the freedom and truthfulness of Harris's writing in his last book meant that his "other fellow" had fully accepted himself, but we find no evidence that Joe Harris's personality had undergone any radical changes in his next-to-last year. His search for a complete and viable identity continued until the end.

In May 1908 *Uncle Remus's Magazine* merged with *The Home Magazine* of Indianapolis; and, although *Uncle Remus's The Home Magazine* now reached two hundred thousand people a month, Harris's journalism days were soon to be over. He had begun to be quite listless in May and early June; and, when a doctor's examination disclosed acute nephritis and cirrhosis of the liver, he was ordered to bed. About this time Harris indicated a desire to speak with Father Jackson, Essie's pastor, to ask to be baptized into the Catholic faith. The priest later recalled that Harris expressed his regret over not having taken the step earlier; characteristically, he was afraid that some might now think he joined the Church "because he was dying."[51] Perhaps Harris's discomfort in public had kept him from becoming a churchgoer; but, whatever the reason, his espousal of the faith was welcomed and understood by his family.

Harris lingered close to death for his last ten days; and, when uremic poisoning set in, he slipped quietly into unconsciousness and died on Friday, July 3, 1908. Harris had once observed that "Humor is an excellent thing to live by, and all things being equal, an excellent thing to die by."[52] With wonderful consistency of character, then, Joel Chandler Harris made his last comment before he lost consciousness. When Julian asked how he felt, he replied with a little of the old twinkle still in his eye: "I am about the extent of a tenth of a gnat's eyebrow better."

III *Posthumous Works*

In addition to his two late novels, *The Bishop and the Booger-man* and *The Shadow Between His Shoulder-Blades,* Harris's family arranged for the posthumous publication of some remaining Uncle Remus tales that Harris for various reasons had not bothered to collect in book form. *Uncle Remus and the Little Boy* appeared in 1910,[53] *Uncle Remus Returns* in 1918,[54] and a reprinting of "Uncle Remus's Wonder Story" entitled *The Witch Wolf* was published in 1921;[55] and Thomas English edited *Seven Tales of Uncle Remus* in 1948.[56] This same year, the centennial of Harris's birth, saw the first of a series of new American editions of Harris's works.[57] The most important of these, Houghton Mifflin's *Favorite Uncle Remus* and their *Complete Tales of Uncle Remus,* the latter edited in 1955 by Richard Chase, realized a combined sale of seventy-five thousand volumes by 1966;[58] Harris's writings have also been translated into more than twenty foreign languages. Clearly, the claims by Harris's contemporaries about his universality were no exaggeration.

CHAPTER 3

The Major Uncle Remus Books

I Uncle Remus and the Critics

HARRIS'S fame would be secure today had he written no other volumes after *Uncle Remus: His Songs and His Sayings* (1880). Later collections of Remus stories reveal more fully elaborated portraits of Uncle Remus and the little boy, an expanded cast of storytellers, and more sophisticated sequencing and structuring of tales. Furthermore, "Free Joe," "Mingo," *The Chronicles of Aunt Minervy Ann,* and other writings are also accomplished works of imaginative literature. Despite these later developments, the three things in Harris that popular readers and critics alike have most frequently praised — his portrait of the old plantation South; one of the world's most enduring characters, Uncle Remus; and Brer Rabbit the archetypal trickster — are fully realized in Harris's first book.

Harris's introduction to *Uncle Remus* reveals the personal perspectives that informed not only his first volume but most of the Remus books to come. As I have indicated, he sought to give "vivid hints" of the humor and the "really poetic imagination of the negro" and to present a "by no means unattractive phase of negro character" that had not been portrayed by Mrs. Stowe.[1] Yet he did not intend for his book to be received only as a volume of humor, even though Appleton's was listing it among their humorous publications. The purpose of the book was "perfectly serious," wrote Harris, because he was trying to preserve the old plantation way of life which had been lost when the Civil War was lost and because he was seeking to give a dialectically and psychologically authentic portrait of the old-time Negro. Harris modestly acknowledged in his introduction the attention that his newspaper tales had attracted among folklorists, but he said it would be "presumptive" in him to try to account for the origins of the tales. He felt, however, that they were probably of African derivation.

Harris's most interesting observations in his introduction, at least in light of what recent sociological critics have found in the Uncle Remus tales as a whole, concern the allegorical implications of the fables. Harris admitted that allegorical interpretations of the Southern Negroes' tales were by no means "unreasonable." After all, "it needs no scientific investigation to show why [the Negro] selects as his hero the weakest and most harmless of all animals, and brings him out victorious in contests with the bear, the wolf, and the fox." And then Harris adds, "It is not virtue that triumphs, but helplessness; it is not malice, but mischievousness."

This statement is too sweeping, for Brer Rabbit definitely acts out of pure malice in more than one story in the first Remus volume, and in several later tales as well. The earlier statement is suggestive, however, for here Harris comments, albeit indirectly and cautiously, upon the condition of the Negro during slavery. Harris's statement is tentative for two reasons. In the first place, Harris, a postwar meliorist and a fledgling author, did not want to make an unqualified critique of black or white racial attitudes. In the second place, he could not be entirely certain about the racial themes concealed in the animal fables. But he did see in the urbane and resourceful trickster-figure of Brer Rabbit a projection of the Negro's desire to realize power or prowess in a world controlled by a stronger race. An inveterate practical joker himself and an avid supporter of the underdog, Harris also identified instinctively with the dazzling improvisational style of his rabbit-hero.

Harris knew that the tales that he had so carefully sought to verify were technically not his but the Negroes', and he acknowledges again his uncertainty and ambivalency about the stories' final meanings on the last page of the introduction. He suggests that the reader suspend his disbelief and allow Remus a double-identity of sorts when he tells his legends. Those unfamiliar with plantation life should imagine that the "myth-stories" are told to a little boy by an old Negro "who appears to be venerable enough to have lived during the period which he describes — who has nothing but pleasant memories of the discipline of slavery — and who has all the prejudices of caste and pride of family that were the natural results of the system."

In other words, Remus tells his stories during the postwar period but attempts to recreate in them the atmosphere of the old times when Remus himself was younger and still a slave. If the reader "can imagine all this," Harris continues, "he will find little difficulty in appreciating and sympathizing with the air of affectionate superiority which Uncle Remus assumes as he proceeds to unfold the mysteries of plantation lore to a little child who is the product of that practical reconstruction which has been going on to some extent since the war in spite of the politicians." This last comment alludes to the 1877 *Constitution* story "Uncle Remus as a Rebel," revised for *Uncle Remus* as "A Story of the War," in which the little boy is identified as the offspring of a Southern woman who married a Yankee soldier.

In claiming in almost the same breath that Uncle Remus had "nothing but pleasant memories" of slavery, and yet had an air of "affectionate superiority" in his dealings with the little boy, Harris reveals his awareness of black role-playing and artful indirection around whites, as well as his own prejudice for the old slavery era — when blacks were, essentially, kept in their place and were presumed to be content with the system of things. As Paul Laurence Dunbar later said of his race in his poem "We Wear the Mask," the Negro hides his suffering from white people by wearing a mask "that grins and lies." Thus Uncle Remus unfolds "the mysteries of plantation lore" to his young listener with an ironic half-humorous and half-melancholic twinkle in his eyes — one which even Harris himself did not fully understand. For, in his tales of Brer Rabbit's cockiness and trickery, Remus is testing the limits of perception and the racial sensitivity of his old as well as young white audience.

Whatever Harris's awareness of his stories' sociological content, his instinctive feel for the ways of animals and men, and his sense of the comic and ironic nature of experience, clearly struck a resonant chord with popular readers and scholars alike. It can be said that the Remus tales became classics the moment they were published because they were both original and universal and because Harris wrote so effortlessly and succinctly. *Uncle Remus* and the volumes that followed, especially *Nights with Uncle Remus* (1883) and *Uncle Remus and His Friends* (1892), precipitated three basic schools of scholarship and criticism, each of which has grown to considerable proportions over the years. Reviewing for a moment the major contributions of the literary and historical scholars, the folklorists and linguists, and the sociological and psychological critics puts Harris's writings, and his own comments on his art, in a larger perspective.

The literary and historical critics, who have uniformly praised Harris's art and social sensitivity, have termed his Remus tales unique and destined for a "permanent place" in American literature. Twain, Cable, Howells, Thomas Nelson Page, Hamlin Garland, and other literary lights of the day lauded Harris's portraits of the old plantation era; and, as early as 1887, his contributions were being acknowledged in standard American literary histories.[2] The first extensive biographical and critical assessment of Harris was William M. Baskervill's in 1896, and ten years after Harris's death Wiggins's and Julia Collier Harris's full biographies brought the essential facts of his life and the background of his works into public view.[3] Francis Pendleton Gaines, Walter Blair, Thomas H. English, and Jay B. Hubbell wrote discriminating commentaries in the 1930s, 1940s, and 1950s about Harris's works in the light of his milieu, personality, and moral and social views.[4] In 1956, Harris scholarship took a classical turn with Ellen Douglass Leyburn's study of Harris's allegorical artistry in comparison to the work of other animal fabulists from Caxton to Orwell.[5] In the last fifteen years Wade Hall, Jay Martin, and Paul Cousins have reexamined the relationship between Harris's writings and his times.[6]

The folklorists have found in Harris's Uncle Remus tales the most important gathering of Negro folk material in the nineteenth century. Although Harris overlooked important Negro tales such as the "Old Marster and John" cycle and despite the fact that the Uncle Remus–little boy framing device was his own artistic addition, his amazingly accurate ear for dialect and inflection and his care in verifying his animal stories before publishing them have continued to impress the professional folklorists.[7] Since the body of research on Harris's folklore is considerable, I shall identify only major trends and scholars here.

In 1881, T. F. Crane, who published the first important essay on Harris as a folklorist,[8] discussed European, Amazonian, and African parallels to the Remus tales; and he prophetically called for an awakening of interest in Negro lore in America. Within a few years, other collections of Negro folklore were being published;[9] and black American culture had suddenly become an important new area for formal research. Crane followed Harris in stating that Africa was the most likely source for the Remus type of animal tale, but Joseph Jacobs introduced in 1888 his theory that India was the original home of the Remus stories.[10] For among the Játakas, or Buddhist birth-stories of ancient India, are tales that feature the hare in a primary role and the stick-fast and five-fold attack motifs so prominent in the tar-baby tale: the two hands, followed by the feet and then by the head, are all caught in a sticky substance.

The newly launched *Journal of American Folk-Lore* and other periodicals immediately began publishing essays arguing for or against the African and Indian theories of origin for the tar-baby story and other Remus tales; in fact, the "war" among the folklorists over the central sources of the Remus tales continues until our present day. Although Aurelio M. Espinosa, in a series of articles across three decades, Ruth Cline, and others have generally followed Jacobs's Indian theory,[11] F. M. Warren, Adolf Gerber, W. Norman Brown, and Elsie Clews Parsons have stressed European and African sources or parallels.[12] In recent essays, William D. Piersen and D. J. M. Muffett suggest that, as African folklore is more thoroughly studied and classified, American Negro tales will probably become more clearly tied to African fables.[13] Although Harris the amateur folklorist may in time be proved correct in his feeling that the Remus tales were of African origin, a major unanswered question is the extent to which black American storytellers modified or reinterpreted in the light of their own condition as slaves the African or European stories that they heard. The more deeply we probe the symbolical meanings of the tales, the more connections we find with black American experience.[14]

Harris's ability to differentiate black and white Southern dialects impressed George Philip Krapp in the 1920s, and Sumner Ives in three studies in the 1950s used Harris as a model for developing a theory of literary dialect.[15] But some of the most interesting commentary about Harris merges folkloristic research with sociological investigation. Kathleen Light, for example, contends that Harris lost interest in ethnology and in theories of cultural evolution after publishing *Nights with Uncle Remus* (1883) because he could not reconcile the sophistication and the subtlety of the supposedly more "primitive" African Jack tales with his belief that later generations of Negroes should be more culturally advanced. Forced "to admit a level of black consciousness which threaten[ed] him as a white man," Harris backed away from ethnology in later volumes and instead poked fun at the folklorists.[16]

Several important studies have been made of Brer Rabbit's role as a trickster. There are obvious parallels between the Remus stories and the cycles of trickster tales that are universal among the world's peoples; yet, at the same time, as Harris himself implied, the rabbit's trickery seems to represent specific psychological and social themes in pre–Civil War American Negro culture in the South. In his essay in the Funk and Wagnalls *Dictionary of Folklore,* Benjamin Albert Botkin points out that the hare is often cast in the role of trickster in the folklore of India and Africa and in that of the American Indian; and, paralleling Harris's own thoughts, Botkin observes that among the American Negroes the rabbit's use of cunning and deception is "in line with the universal tendency on the part of oppressed people to identify themselves with the weaker and triumphant animal in the pitting of brains against brute force and superior strength."[17] Louise Dauner, Paul Radin, and Carl Jung discuss the trickster-figure as a product of mankind's mythopoeic imagination; and they regard the amorality and the creative-destructive dichotomy of the trickster as universal instincts.[18] Largely because of the celebrated tar-baby tale, Brer Rabbit is probably the best-known trickster in the world's folklore. Stella Brookes catalogues eighty-three Remus tales in which the rabbit tricks the other creatures, and twenty-nine tales in which other animals function as tricksters.[19] Among modern black city-dwellers, the Brer Rabbit trickster cycle lives on but in a somewhat modified character: the rabbit becomes the "hard man" of agility, meanness, and strength who has the ability "to revolt in the face of authority and possible death."[20]

Overtly sociological approaches to Harris began in the 1930s with the work of the black author Sterling Brown. Brown thought Uncle Remus one of the classic characters in American literature, but he still saw him as a stereotypical portrait of the prewar contented slave, an image that influenced later literary portraits of the black man.[21] A third of a century later Brown's views were still being echoed by black critics. Darwin T. Turner, for example, acknowledged the mental, physical, and emotional differences among Harris's Negro characters; but he viewed them as essentially sexless, devoted, and unobtrusive "darkies" serving patriarchal masters in a utopian plantation society.[22]

Other writers, including black scholars like J. Mason Brewer,[23] have found the Uncle Remus tales to be intriguing symbolical studies that portray the Negro slave's sense of his own condition.

Critics disagree, however, about the degree of Harris's racial awareness in the tales. Daniel G. Hoffman and Lyle Glazier believe that Uncle Remus is in many ways a minstrel portrait of the black slave but that Brer Rabbit's trickery, which Harris probably did not appreciate fully, represents allegorically the Negro's struggle for survival and his indomitable spirit.[24] Robert Bone argues persuasively that Harris's tales are distinctly Afro-American; in them Harris consciously or unconsciously portrayed the black man's symbolical projection of the harsh, antipastoral world of Negro slavery in which an "outlaw survival code" prevailed.[25]

In a suggestive article, Bernard Wolfe contends that, although Harris identified with the social struggle of the Negro and was impressed with the black man's creative ability, he remained a victim of the usual Southern prejudices and was reluctant to face the racial themes of his Remus tales. Real malevolence toward the white race[26] is concealed for Wolfe beneath Uncle Remus's smiling countenance and symbolized in the behavior of his hero Brer Rabbit. Jesse Bier, on the other hand, feels that "in his depths" Harris was secretly opposed to the Southern code of gentility and pride, as well as to the Northern code of victory and rapacity. Thus Harris's amoral Uncle Remus tales are perhaps the most "cynical" pieces in all of American humor, for they propound an "ethic of success at any cost, placing the rabbit (the wily, unreconstructed south) against the fox (the predatory north)," and permit the rabbit any means of survival. Brer Rabbit's deviousness and his power to endure also typify the psychology of the Negro, whom Harris respects.[27] And, as Michael Flusche suggests, there is evidence that Harris's own deep-seated insecurity and personal negativism underlie the superficially comic surface of his tales.[28]

Although critics do not agree about the final meaning of the Uncle Remus stories and although Harris himself was apparently uncertain about their implications, Louis Rubin's may be the most balanced and viable perspective. In two recent articles he observes that Harris was a segregationist who saw the black man as socially and biologically inferior; but, as an artist who himself came from deprived and humble origins, he sympathized with the underdog Negro and admired the black man's hero, the clever and mischievous rabbit. Paralleling some of Jay Martin's ideas, Rubin explains that Harris was a psychologically complex figure; he was a journalist and an optimist on the surface but a "fiercely creative artist" and realist underneath. His Remus tales are not "parables of pro-

test"; instead, they show Harris's humane and imaginative attempt
to comprehend "the situation of the black man in a society made
up, so far as he was concerned, of foxes and wolves who possessed
all the money, the education, the power, the advantages."[29]

II   Uncle Remus: His Songs and His Sayings *(1880)*

Harris's first book, *Uncle Remus: His Songs and His Sayings,* is
a miscellaneous anthology of the Old South; for, in addition to
thirty-four Uncle Remus folk tales, it contains seventy plantation
maxims and proverbs, ten Negro songs, the revised Uncle Remus
war-tale, "A Story of the War," and twenty-one sketches featuring
the "other" Uncle Remus — the Atlanta resident. The loose structure of *Uncle Remus* can be credited to the fact that Harris, at
Appleton's suggestion, was collecting the several kinds of material
he had been publishing in the *Constitution* and was adding to it in
various ways. Among Uncle Remus's "Songs" are included the
celebrated "Revival Hymn" as well as representative work songs,
plantation play-songs, and religious songs. And Harris also prints a
humorous serenade and a more philosophical song about the
mutability of life.

Uncle Remus's wisdom as a plantation seer is effectively presented in his proverbial sayings, which provide an index to his composite character as it is more fully displayed in the Atlanta sketches
and in the framing devices surrounding the animal fables. Both the
Putnam County uncle and his Atlanta cousin share similar views
about the value of work, right behavior, and simple endurance in
the face of trouble. In fact, we could argue that, in the transcribed
proverbs, Harris synthesizes and helps to promulgate an image of
the Negro that influenced not only Thomas Nelson Page's portraits
of black character but also those of Twain and William Faulkner. It
is not hard to imagine Twain's loyal "Nigger Jim," or Faulkner's
conscientious Aunt Dilsey observing with Uncle Remus that
"Nigger dat gets hurt wukkin oughter show de skyars," that
"Sleepin' in de fence-cornder don't fetch Chrismus in de kitchen,"
or that "Ha'nts don't bodder longer hones' folk, but you better go
'roun' de graveyard." Dilsey and Jim also knew firsthand the
ordeals of deprivation and the quiet rewards of endurance that
Uncle Remus aphorizes:

De proudness un a man don't count w'en his head's cold.
Better de gravy dan no grease 'tall.
Dem w'at eats kin say grace.
Ef you bleedzd ter eat dirt, eat clean dirt.

Repeatedly in the Atlanta sketches Remus counsels his Negro brethren to achieve dignity, pride, and integrity as a race; the question of black canniness around whites is more carefully veiled in the allegorical tales that the country Remus tells. The city-dwelling Remus reproves hypocritical black parishioners in "Uncle Remus's Church Experience," sleek but irresponsible Savannah boys in "Uncle Remus and the Savannah Darkey," and loafers in "Turnip Salad as a Text." In "Race Improvement," Uncle Remus is glad to see that blacks have lost a little of the arrogance they showed right after freedom came and are now becoming more conscientious citizens: " 'You slap de law onter a nigger a time or two, an' larn 'im dat he's got fer to look atter his own rashuns an' keep out'n udder fokes's chick'n-coops, an' sorter coax 'im inter de idee dat he's got ter feed 'is own chilluns, an' I be blessed ef you ain't got 'im on risin' groun'.' " Remus's point is that blacks are going to have to improve their image and their sense of responsibility before real social progress can be made. The Atlanta sketches are, of course, not free of Harris's own prejudices; for, even though Harris hoped that educating the Negro would solve many of his problems, he often wondered about the ultimate educability of a "primitive" race. Perhaps the black man was best suited for physical labor; for, as Remus laments, " 'Put a spellin'-book in a nigger's han's, en right den en dar' you loozes a plow-hand.' "

While the scene and the format of the city sketches vary — Remus is overheard chastising blacks on the street, or complaining about the times to the *Constitution* staff, or sharing his experiences with a crony — the structure of the animal legends is relatively stable and predictable throughout all the Uncle Remus volumes. The scene opens at Remus's hearth in his cabin behind "the big house." Typically, he is doing a small domestic task, such as threading a needle, or fishing a hot yam out of the fire, or sharpening a knife on his palm. The little boy is at his knee, and either one of the boy's comments or a remark by Remus himself puts the old man " 'in min' of de time dat Brer Rabbit....' " At this point, the cabin scene dissolves into a scene on " 'de big road' " where Brer Rabbit and Brer Fox, or another of the stronger creatures, pause to exchange superficial social greetings: "Heyo .. how you come on?" Soon the two creatures have agreed to a contest, "partnership," or other activity that almost inevitably results in Brer Rabbit's outwitting his rival. Then the cabin scene reappears, and Uncle Remus responds to the little boy's question, for he usually has at least one question, with a moral tag or epigrammatic comment.

Since Harris typically interlocks his tales, each of the Remus books can be considered a complete narrative cycle. Within each volume, though, Harris includes different types of folk tales. *Uncle Remus,* for example, contains two stories about witches and conjurations, as well as six etiological tales that account for features of the natural landscape or animals' or humans' physical characteristics (how crawfish caused the Great Flood, why the possum has no hair on his tail, and other motifs). Of the remaining tales in Harris's first book, four cast Brer Tarrypin as the trickster; in one, Brer Fox plays the role; in the other twenty-three stories, Brer Rabbit is the archetypal trickster-hero.

Harris's narrative frame is a deceptively thin vehicle for a cumulative portrait of Uncle Remus that is substantial and complex; but the little boy, who serves primarily as a foil to Remus, also develops his character as the cycles of tales progress. By the end of the first book, Remus has acquired all the important characteristics that the later volumes would reiterate. He is nearly eighty years old; he is bespectacled and white-haired; but he is still strong and tall in frame, vigorous in his gestures, and proud of his position as a family retainer. In the story frames in *Nights with Uncle Remus* (1883) and *Daddy Jake* (1889), Harris explains more fully the reasons for Remus's pride of station. When he was younger, he had been the strongest and most versatile of the slaves and had commanded not only their respect but that of the household by virtue of his example and prowess. Uncle Remus is superior and overbearing around the lower-class "River" Negroes, who occasionally visit the big house, and around " 'dem house niggers,' " who go about " 'wid der han's en der mouf open, en w'at one don't ketch de tother one do.' " Despite his criticism of the house servants, however, Remus wants the little boy to bring him food or supplies from the kitchen whenever possible — and he can also be quite devious in obtaining handouts. In *Uncle Remus and His Friends* (1892), we also learn that Remus had in time married and had reared two children.

Harris's gift for characterization and his sensitivity to the psychology of human behavior are revealed in the interplay between Uncle Remus and the boy, as well as in the fables themselves. It is obvious that Remus loves his white listener as much as the boy loves him, and at times the old man calls the boy " 'Honey' " and openly caresses or holds him. Fatherless himself, Harris must have projected something of his own concept of a concerned and loving father into his portrait of Remus. In depicting this innocent and spontaneous love between a black man and a white boy, Harris also writes another chapter in Leslie Fiedler's study of chaste interracial male love in America.[30] James Fenimore Cooper's Natty Bumppo and Chingachgook and Herman Melville's Ishmael and Queequeg are earlier figures in this tradition, but the relationship between the little boy and Uncle Remus may have directly influenced Twain's portraits of Huck and Jim in *Huckleberry Finn* (1884).

As would be the case with Jim, moreover, Uncle Remus is not afraid to chastise the boy he loves. At times, his criticism can be mild and indirect, as at the beginning of "A Story about the Little Rabbits." When Remus emphasizes how well-behaved and obedient the little rabbits were around their parents and how they also did not have any smut on their noses, the boy involuntarily scrubs his nose with his coatsleeve. When the lad has been particularly mischievous, Uncle Remus sits quietly and sighs, or he openly refuses to start a tale, as a sign of his displeasure; for Remus knows how to let recollected sin do its work. After his young listener has grown sufficiently uneasy, Remus explains that boys should not tattle on their younger brothers (legend XIX), should not chunk rocks at the chickens, turn a puppy loose in the pig pen, or fling stones on Remus's own roof (legend VII). Furthermore, Uncle Remus's instinctive class-consciousness and pride are projected into his criticism of the boy's playing with the disreputable Favers children (legend XXVII). Favers were " 'no 'count 'fo' de war, en de wa'n't no 'count endurin' er de war, en dey ain't no 'count afterwards.' " And " 'w'iles my head's hot,' " Remus concludes, " 'you ain't gwineter go mixin' up yo'se'f wid de riff-raff er creashun.' "

Harris reveals his psychological perceptivity and his sensitivity to the subtle uses of power by the black man when around white folks in depicting Remus's various strategies for keeping the little boy interested and involved in tales which Remus knows to be fabulous and even preposterous at times. Thus Remus palms off improbable

stories by saying only that he had heard them that way, or that in
the old days that's the way things were. He often purposely draws
attention to a marvelous motif in a story, such as the fact that Brer
Rabbit once walked the big road with a fine bushy tail, in order to
provoke a protest from the boy; then he criticizes those folks that
pretend to know too much. Remus also intentionally stops a tale
just before its conclusion and sends the boy to bed, and the next
time they are together he expresses surprise that he had not finished
the story. A more conventional strategy is his starting a tale, ter-
minating it immediately, and observing that the boy will not be
interested.

Remus is a master storyteller and knows it, and he cannot stand
to be interrupted by skeptical questions or by irrelevant comments
from his young listener. For example, when the boy wants to know
what name " 'de man' " had in legend XXIX, Remus says he will
have to hunt up one of the new breed of Negroes and ask him. The
old man's most complex reaction to the boy's questioning spirit
comes in legend XX when Uncle Remus realizes that the boy has
indeed caught him in a contradiction: Brer Wolf had died in sketch
XIII, but Remus has now reintroduced him. At first Remus turns a
frown of "scorn and indignation" upon the boy; but then he partially relents and adopts a pose of "Christian resignation" by complaining to an imaginary third party about children that know more
than older folks and little boys who should soon be off to bed.
When Remus next observes that a certain little chap had grown up
so fast that he would no longer need a whip that he was braiding for
him, he brings the boy to tears; at this juncture, Remus sees that his
display of power and his need to make the boy feel guilty have gone
too far. He apologizes and caresses the boy's hand, but Remus still
has to be coaxed into resuming his story.

The animal fables themselves allow Harris greater opportunity,
of course, to display his versatility as a portrayer of character. Yet it
is important to see that the stories and their frames reinforce each
other. The stories dramatize and put into allegorical form the more
subtle tensions between the races that the framing devices so often
display; furthermore, in seeking to make the young white boy
admire the urbane but rascally Brer Rabbit in his triumphs over the
fox, wolf, and bear, Uncle Remus is rhetorically and symbolically
stating the case for the needed realignment in the social structure
and mores of white society. In the allegory of the tales, the stronger
race of creatures is forced to recognize and respect the upstart,

clever hero of the supposedly weaker race and to give him room in their social system. At the same time, however, Remus saw and was troubled by the backlash that could result when the black man, freed of slavery, began to make his presence felt. For Brer Rabbit's unfettered mischievousness can get him into trouble, and his penchant for violence can leave a disturbing aftertaste in the mouth. Archetypally, Brer Rabbit's escapades show the pleasure and the pain, the creation and the destruction, that follow in the trickster's wake.

The most famous of the animal fables, the tar-baby story, serves well as a paradigm for Harris's technique and vision. Although the tale proper is told in legends II and IV, the story is actually part of a subtly interconnected series of four tales that Harris uses to open his book. "Uncle Remus Initiates the Little Boy," the first tale, is an "initiation story" in more than one way. It introduces the reader to the little boy and to the weather-beaten old narrator and his subtle rhetorical devices, and it initiates both the boy and the reader in the wily ways of Brer Rabbit and his chief antagonist throughout the several Remus volumes, Brer Fox. But the first story also establishes the controlling allegorical motifs of voracity and potential destructiveness that underlie ironic friendship among the " 'creeturs' " and of the superiority of shiftiness over honesty as a survival technique.

In this story, Brer Fox, who has been trying unsuccessfully to catch Brer Rabbit, meets his rival " 'a lopin' up de big road, lookin' des ez plump, en ez fat, en ez sassy ez a Moggin hoss in a barley-patch.' " Brer Fox, who attempts to use friendship as a ruse to put his foe off-guard, says that Brer B'ar had been complaining that the fox and the rabbit had not decided to live "naberly." Brer Rabbit suspects a trap and, when he invites Brer Fox over for dinner, keeps a sharp lookout. He spots the fox lurking outside the house, locks the door, and sings a song to let Brer Fox know indirectly that he has been found out. The next day the fox sends word that he has been sick and asks Brer Rabbit to have a chicken dinner at his place. When Brer Rabbit realizes that he is to be the dinner, he declines the invitation on the grounds that he cannot eat chicken unless it is seasoned with calamus root; and the rabbit gallops home. Remus concludes the first tale: " 'En Brer Fox ain't never kotch 'im yit, en w'at's mo', honey, he ain't gwineter.' "

One of the most subtle patterns in the Remus tales is the creatures' careful avoidance of direct accusations of each other for potential or actual misdeeds. The fox hides his voracity; and, in later tales, the rabbit conceals his retributive acts behind a veneer of sociality or oblique statements. As social allegories, the Remus tales are discerning studies in racial pride among blacks, as well as whites, and in the subtleties of role-playing.

The uncatchable rabbit is, however, temporarily caught in the second tale, "The Wonderful Tar-Baby Story." After being fooled by the calamus root trick, Brer Fox fashions the tar-baby out of turpentine and tar and places it in the big road to trap Brer Rabbit. " 'Tar-Baby, she sot dar, she did,' " says Remus, " 'en Brer Fox, he lay low.' " When the rabbit comes along in a typically sassy mood, he gives the usual social greetings to this new neighbor: "Mawnin'! ... nice wedder dis mawnin'!" Harris's speech rhythms become more insistent:

> "Tar-Baby ain't sayin' nothin', en Brer Fox, he lay low.
> " 'How duz yo' sym'tums seem ter segashuate?' sez Brer Rabbit, sezee.
> "Brer Fox, he wink his eye slow, en lay low, en de Tar-Baby, she ain't sayin' nothing'."

Growing more and more irritated with the unneighborliness of his new acquaintance, Brer Rabbit hollers louder in case the tar-baby is deaf; he accuses it of being "stuck up," which proves to be an unintentional pun; and then he finally strikes it with his fist to teach it to act "'spectubble" to folks. The whole time, of course, " 'Tar-Baby ain't sayin' nothin',' " and " 'Brer Fox, he lay low.' " The story closes in the familiar way: Brer Rabbit is entirely "stuck up" (both hands, both feet, and his head are caught in the tar), and Brer Fox rolls on the ground and laughs over the fact that this time Brer Rabbit cannot find an excuse for declining the dinner invitation.

When the little boy asks whether the fox ate the rabbit, Remus displays his own wiliness around white folks by saying, " 'Dat's all de fur de tale goes.... He mout, en den again he moutent. Some say Jedge B'ar come along en loosed 'im — some say he didn't.' " Then Remus hears Miss Sally calling and sends the boy off. In a typically subtle use of power, Uncle Remus keeps his white listener waiting several days — in the interim, he relates an etiological tale about why Brer Possum plays dead — before concluding the tar-baby story. In his celebrated use of reverse psychology, Brer Rabbit talks " 'mighty 'umble' " and tells Brer Fox to burn him, or hang him, or drown him, or skin him, just as long as Brer Fox does not throw him in the brier-patch. The brier-patch is precisely where he ends up, of course; and, after combing the tar out of his hair, Brer Rabbit resumes his sassy posture and taunts Brer Fox with a fact of nature: he was "Bred en bawn in a brier-patch!"

As Remus observes to the little boy in legend IV, Brer Rabbit was a " 'monstus soon creetur' " who was at " 'de head er de gang' " when any racket was going on. Frequently he uses his trickery to obtain food and other necessities of life. Yet, being an inveterate prankster, Brer Rabbit cannot stand it when the neighborhood is quiet. A compulsive disturber of the peace, he vexes the stronger race of creatures and shows, allegorically, that the black man must be given room in the white social structure. In "Mr. Rabbit Grossly Deceives Mr. Fox," for example, Brer Rabbit shows off for " 'Miss Meadows en de gals' " by pretending to be sick and by conning Brer Fox into putting on a saddle and carrying him to the girls' party horseback fashion. In front of Miss Meadows's place, Brer Rabbit digs a pair of concealed spurs into the fox's sides to complete his joke with an appropriate flourish; the subservient creature, long ridden upon, here literally rides upon his stronger foe. The story ends with Brer Rabbit's sitting among the gals and jauntily smoking a cigar, " 'same ez a town man.' " Harris intentionally keeps the exact profession of Miss Meadows and her friends ambiguous throughout the Remus volumes; it may, in fact, be the oldest profession in the world. At any rate, the fox, the wolf, and Brer Rabbit, who is a bachelor in some stories and family man in others, spend a good deal of time " 'co'tin en sparklin' . . . mo' samer dan folks' " and demonstrating their manly prowess for Miss Meadows and the gals.

As I indicated earlier, in several of the tales Remus seems to warn allegorically that too much mischievousness on the part of the upstart rabbit can be counterproductive; too strong a push for racial upward mobility and progress can backfire. Brer Rabbit barely escaped the tar-baby trap, and in a few tales his arrogant manner and his pranking do in fact catch up with him. For instance, Brer Tarrypin uses some of the rabbit's own brand of trickery in the Uncle Remus version of the tortoise and the hare story, "Mr. Rabbit Finds His Match at Last." When Brer Rabbit brags that he is the faster runner, Brer Tarrypin challenges him to a race. Placing his family members at the various mileposts, Brer Tarrypin cuts through the crowd to the finish-line and declares himself the winner.

A more psychologically compelling tale is "Mr. Rabbit Meets

His Match Again,'' in which Brer Rabbit welches on an agreement
with Brer Buzzard to be partners in finding food: Brer Buzzard has
nothing to show for his efforts, but Brer Rabbit keeps his considerable gathering of supplies a secret. When Brer Buzzard suspects
that the rabbit is holding out on him, he offers to fly him to see a
gold mine that he claims to have discovered; when the buzzard
takes him instead to a deserted island in the middle of the river,
Brer Rabbit gets scared and offers to divide fairly what he has
already found. '' 'Brer Rabbit,' '' observes Uncle Remus, '' 'he
walk weak in de knees a mont' atterwuds.' '' A variation of this
psychological pattern is found in the etiological legend XXV, in
which the aggressive rabbit asks Brer Fox for some of his fresh-
caught fish — and the fox tells him to fish with his bushy tail for his
own dinner. By morning, his tail has been eaten off, or, more symbolically, his ego emasculated. Furthermore, the sins of the fathers
are visited upon the children and upon the children's children; for,
ever since Brer Rabbit's fishing adventure, rabbits have had short
tails.

As Ellen Leyburn has observed, the Uncle Remus tales are
effective as satiric allegory because Harris makes us appreciate
simultaneously both the human and the animal traits of Brer
Rabbit and the other creatures. Brer Rabbit is real both as an animal and as a person, and in his knavery he continually satirizes the
gullibility, pride, and greed of the other creatures.[31] Yet Brer Rabbit
has his own weaknesses and excesses, too; he can be overbearing in
his pride and cockiness, and at times his love of roguery is mali-
cious and immoral. In "Mr. Rabbit Nibbles Up the Butter," for
example, he steals butter from the supply that he, the fox, and the
possum have agreed to hold in common. Brer Rabbit promises to
find the thief, but in the night he smears butter on the possum's
mouth and paws. Trying to defend himself, Brer Possum suggests
the next morning that the three of them build a fire and each jump
over it; the thief, the heaviest animal, would presumably not be
able to make the jump. Ironically, Brer Rabbit and Brer Fox clear
the blaze, but the luckless possum falls in and dies. In the most
brutal tale in *Uncle Remus,* "The Sad Fate of Mr. Fox," Brer Fox
with a rare act of generosity shows Brer Rabbit how he can jump
into a cow's stomach and get some meat without killing the cow.
But Brer Rabbit purposely gives the beast a fatal cut; and, when
Mr. Man comes along, the rabbit informs him that the fox had
killed his cow. After the man has killed the fox, Brer Rabbit cruelly

takes Brer Fox's head home to Mrs. Fox — and tells her it is nice beef. In the closing episode in the tale, which is reminiscent of a European folk motif, Brer Fox's son discovers to his horror that his own father's head is in the dinner pot.

When the little boy protests the injustice of the possum's death in the earlier story, Uncle Remus explains that in this world lots of folks suffer innocently for others' sins. Since the cheating of the animals, Remus observes at the end of the tortoise-race story, eventually spread to the world of men, men must take care that they are not cheated. Remus does not always insist, however, upon parallels between animal and human behavior; for he states in *Uncle Remus and His Friends* that the creatures, who do not know right from wrong, only take things they need. Yet behind Brer Rabbit's more disconcerting tricks and Remus's pithy comments is concealed Harris's complex vision of reality and of the trickster's role in shaping it either for good or for ill. On the one hand, the trickster works for needed social progress and an expanded definition of freedom. On the other, his overconfidence and his brashness can get him into trouble, and his violent sense of a practical joke on his superiors and his vengefulness can wreak moral and social chaos in our world. A story like "The Awful Fate of Mr. Wolf," in which Brer Rabbit and his family scald the wolf to death because he had been carrying off some of the rabbit children, holds up the spectre of bloodshed and retribution as an allegorical warning to whites and blacks alike about the consequences of racial mistrust or hatred.

III Nights with Uncle Remus: Myths and Legends of the Old Plantation *(1883)*

It is clear from an unpublished manuscript note in the Harris collection at Emory that Harris planned his second volume of Remus tales rather carefully; he was taking his new role as creative writer more seriously now, and his projected book reveals his growing rhetorical and structural artistry. Harris wrote that *Nights with Uncle Remus* would feature an expanded cast of plantation characters: the cook Aunt Tempy and the pert and indecorous house-girl 'Tildy would act as foils to Remus and to Daddy Jack, a friend of Remus's from the Sea Islands who would narrate some Gullah dialect tales. Harris adds that the eighteen tales that he had already written for the *Constitution* would be modified to suit the more ambitious and mature plan of the book.

Harris subsequently wrote a thirty-one page introduction to *Nights with Uncle Remus* in which he further explained his reasons for broadening the scope of his second book. Rather than including primarily Middle Georgia Negro lore, as in the first volume, he wanted to be more representative in the new book and so would draw upon legends and motifs sent in by correspondents from around the South. As I mentioned in Chapter 2, Harris's footnoted introduction also reveals how his interest in comparative folklore had grown since he had published *Uncle Remus* three years earlier. Furthermore, Harris demonstrates even greater linguistic skill in the second book. Not only is Daddy Jack's Gullah speech accurately rendered (Harris prepares the reader for the idiosyncrasies of this dialect by including a glossary of Gullah vocabulary), but Harris even differentiates carefully among the speech patterns and narrative rhythms of the three Middle Georgia blacks — Aunt Tempy, 'Tildy, and Uncle Remus.[32]

While the individual animal stories in *Nights with Uncle Remus* are similar to the fables in the previous book — trickster tales featuring the rabbit as hero, etiological legends, and tales in which creatures other than Brer Rabbit have the major role — the structure of the volume as a whole is more sophisticated. Instead of a single tale, the little boy hears a set of from two to five interlocking stories each time he visits Remus. The frames that surround each story are made fuller as Harris spends more time developing the characters of Remus and his listener, who has now grown a little older and wiser. The fact that Harris also introduces three new characters into the narrative framework of the tales confirms his desire to augment folklore with more of his own art in the second book.

Another notable addition to *Nights with Uncle Remus* is Harris's use of imagery and of mood-building in the story frames themselves. At the beginning of the first and eleventh tales, for example, Harris describes the rainy, overcast days of early winter in Middle Georgia; the leafless trees are stark against the gray sky, water from a leak in the old man's roof drips steadily into a tin pan, and Remus's shadow alternately looms up amid the rafters and fades away as he moves around in front of his fireplace. This kind of descriptive detail helps to give Harris's second collection of stories a richness of texture and a reality of presentation that are often lacking in the more perfunctory frames in *Uncle Remus*. Furthermore, the book's closing sketch, a colorful account of plantation

Christmas festivities, becomes an epiphany of rebirth and renewal that functions in esthetic contrast to the gloomy winter settings of the earlier tales in the volume.

In *Nights,* Uncle Remus continues to use a variety of rhetorical devices to keep his young listener attentive and under his power and to remind him that the presumably less-educated black man nevertheless has truths to impart to the white race. In the fourth story, for instance, Remus introduces one of his pet subjects, the perils of playing with the disreputable Favers children, and warns the boy directly to stay away from them. Indeed, the Favers seem more and more to be an anticipation of Faulkner's Snopses. Remus complains of their bad " 'breedin' en raisin' ' " in comparison to that of Mars John and Sally Abercrombie; old Cajy Favers ended up in the poorhouse; and Jim Favers knows the inside of all the jails in Georgia. Remus adds, " 'Dey allers did hate niggers kase dey aint had none, en dey hates un down ter dis day.' " Remus uses another of his standard techniques for keeping the little boy in line in story XXXIX in which he tells Aunt Tempy and the others, in the boy's presence, that he had promised an acquaintance of his a rabbit-trap if that person would " 'l'arn he behavishness.' "

In stories XXIII and XLIV, Remus again uses guilt as his tactic when he laments that the boy is getting too smart for him and is outgrowing the tales, and that maybe Remus had better get his " 'remoovance papers' " from Miss Sally and head down the big road. Similarly, in tale XLVII Remus poor-mouths himself in comparison to Daddy Jack, who intrigues the boy, and says that he will henceforth retire to the chimney corner and let Jack and the boy go along together. When this lamentation quite naturally provokes a troubled disclaimer from the boy, Remus smiles broadly and proceeds to tell his next story. But Remus is not always harsh or devious with his young listener. Sometimes a quick humorous response to a question is sufficient, as is the case when the young lad queries his use of the term " 'jiblets.' " Some folks call them "jiblets," answers Remus, and some call them "hasletts." But, whatever they are called, " 'You do de namin' ... en I'll do de eatin'.' "

Harris's delightful portraits of Remus's new set of visitors — Daddy Jack, 'Tildy, and Aunt Tempy—are the major literary additions to the second book. As critics have observed, the badinage and the petty jealousies and rivalries among these characters are in part a burlesque of the social structure of white society; yet each of

Remus's black friends is also fully developed as a character and as a storyteller with a distinctive narrative style. Daddy Jack, who is known as African Jack to older Negroes, was brought as a slave to the Sea Islands of Georgia when he was twenty; and, after serving the little boy's family for awhile, he had eventually become the foreman of a South Georgia plantation. Now a weazened, dried-up old man of eighty, he enjoyed visiting the Abercrombie place at Christmastime — especially after he had become enamored of 'Tildy, the house-girl. Jack wants to marry 'Tildy, whom he affectionately calls " 'pidjin-toed,' " but she literally keeps laughing in his face. Remus counsels Jack not to wait under the persimmon tree with his mouth open hoping a persimmon will fall in; he must shake the tree to get results. So Daddy Jack presses his suit even harder in tale XXV, only to have 'Tildy threaten to brain him with a fire-iron. " 'I aint gwine ter have no web-foot nigger follerin' atter me,' " she protests, with a satiric reference to his coastal background. But Remus knows that 'Tildy is more taken with Jack than she will admit; before long, in fact, she is a regular visitor in Remus's cabin despite her warnings of violent consequences should Daddy Jack so much as sit next to her.

The cook at the big house, Aunt Tempy, also becomes a regular visitor, although her official duty is to keep the little boy from getting caught in the middle of Jack's and 'Tildy's pretended warfare. Harris explains that Tempy, who exercised what some blacks felt to be tyrannical authority over the house Negroes, was secretly jealous of Remus, the family's favorite, and vice-versa. Like the creatures in the fables, Remus and Tempy exchange superficially sociable greetings: " 'How you come on, Brer Remus?' " " 'Po'ly, Sis Tempy; en yet I aint complainin'.... How you is...?' " " 'I thank de Lord I'm able to crawl, Brer Remus....' " Yet they usually keep their distance from each other. With a subtle rhetorical touch, Harris uses Aunt Tempy to criticize Remus's hero, Brer Rabbit; she defends the wolf's actions in story XXVII, and she keeps interrupting Remus's narrative with comments about Brer Rabbit's pestering and cockiness. Despite their rivalry, however, Tempy and Remus secretly understand each other, and 'Tildy later kids Tempy that she is actually courting Remus. At the end of the story which Tempy had interrupted so frequently, she says how much she had enjoyed hearing the tale because it had reminded her of the " 'ole times.' " When Remus responds that she is always welcome at his hearth, he also observes, " 'Ole times is about all we got lef'.' " " 'Trufe, too!' " exclaims Tempy. Harris closes the sketch with a sensitive symbolical touch: "and with that she took the child by the hand and went out into the darkness."

The four black characters gradually appreciate each other, but their bantering continues. For one thing, they enjoy listening to each others' animal stories; for, although ostensibly told to entertain the little boy, the tales have communal significance as the four characters rediscover the primacy of the oral folk tradition that underlies their own social history, whether they were born in Middle Georgia, Virginia (as was the case with Remus), or Africa. Although Jack, 'Tildy, and Tempy are initially reticent about narrating tales, Remus's and the boy's persistence, and their own pleasure in seeing the group's response when they do relate a story, draw them out. By the end of the volume, Jack has shared ten Gullah tales; Tempy has told five stories; and 'Tildy, three. Occasionally, Jack or Tempy will narrate a variation of one of Remus's tales (Jack is usually convinced that his version is more authentic or vivid), but young 'Tildy may demonstrate the greatest storytelling talent of all of the narrators, Remus included. Tale XXIX, "A Ghost Story," which Harris had reworked from Mark Twain's outline of the golden-arm ghost tale, is told with great effect by 'Tildy. At the climactic moment when the ghost-woman in the tale jumps at the man who had stolen her money, 'Tildy springs at Daddy Jack and hollers, " 'You got my money!' " Jack collapses in fright, and 'Tildy observes triumphantly, " 'Dar, now! I know'd I'd git even wid de ole vilyun. Come a-callin' me pidgin-toed!' "

Daddy Jack's "Cutta Cord-La!" is also a clever tale, but it is more so because it features dialect-within-dialect. In Gullah, Jack explains how Brer Rabbit reneged on an agreement with Brer Wolf to kill his own grandmother when food supplies for the two animals ran low; Wolf had previously contributed his grandmother to the common pot, and he now angrily goes looking for Granny Rabbit. He discovers that Brer Rabbit has concealed her in a tree and has arranged a signal to indicate when she should pull up her daily food basket. The key words are "Jutta cord-la," but Brer Wolf can only manage " 'Shoot-a cord-la,' " to which the grandmother will not respond. After he has gone to the blacksmith to have his voice smoothed out with a hot poker, he succeeds in saying " 'Jutta.' " When the grandmother begins to haul him up in her basket, Brer Rabbit comes by and shouts " 'Cutta cord-la!' "; Granny cuts the rope; and the wolf falls and breaks his neck.

Uncle Remus's best performance in *Nights* is the often-anthologized "The Moon in the Mill-Pond." The little boy had caught Remus asleep in his chair and snoring, but the old storyteller would only admit to having had his head back watching a bat's " 'flutterments' " and thinking about some " 'mighty quare' " notions. " 'De Bat put me in min' er folks,' " Remus continues, " 'en folks put me in min' er de creeturs.' " He says there were times when all the creatures would " 'segashuate tergedder' " with no disputes and when Brer Rabbit even looked as if he were going to reform. But true to his nature as a trickster, the more peaceful it was, the more restless Brer Rabbit got, until finally he and Brer Tarrypin decided to have some fun. Brer Rabbit invited everyone to a moonlight fishing frolic at the mill-pond, and he made sure that Miss Meadows and the gals would be there to watch. Then Remus slides into one of his delightful narrative rhythms as he explains that " 'Brer B'ar 'low he gwine ter fish fer mud-cats,' " and Brer Wolf " 'gwine ter fish fer horney heads,' " and Brer Fox " 'gwine ter fish fer peerch fer de ladies,' " and Brer Tarrypin " 'gwine ter fish fer minners,' " and Brer Rabbit, with a wink at Brer Tarrypin, " 'low he gwine ter fish fer suckers.' " But Brer Rabbit soon says there can be no fishing that night because the moon has fallen into the water. When the creatures see the moon's image swaying in the bottom of the pond and agree with Brer Rabbit that they should borrow Mr. Mud-Turtle's net and seine out the moon, Brer Tarrypin adds to their incentive by passing along the traditional belief that anyone who can fetch the moon out of the water will find a pot of gold.

One by one each of the creatures wades into the pond until he gets water in his ears, and then he steps off over his head and dunks himself. The gals all laugh at the ridiculous spectacle, and Brer Rabbit tells the other animals to go home and get dry clothes. Then he adds: "I hear talk dat de moon'll bite at a hook ef you take fools fer baits, en I lay dat's de onliest way fer ter ketch 'er." Remus ends his story with another perfect narrative and rhetorical rhythm: " 'Brer Fox en Brer Wolf en Brer B'ar went drippin' off, en Brer Rabbit en Brer Tarrypin, dey went home wid de gals.' "

The Christmas epiphany that closes *Nights with Uncle Remus* draws together several narrative and thematic patterns. First, 'Tildy and Jack are married down in the "quarters." As 'Tildy discovered, she not only wanted to take care of old Daddy Jack but had grown tired of having him follow her around; thus " 'I bleedzd

ter marry 'im fer git rid un 'im.' '' In the second place, the
Christmas dancing and the singing celebration in chapter LXXI are
not only symbolical of renewal and rebirth but also suggest the
growing cultural sensitization that both the little boy and the reader
have been undergoing, at Remus's hands, throughout the book. We
can begin to appreciate the old plantation Negroes' joy at the
Christmas pageant because we have now learned something of their
folklore and of their ways as a people.

IV Daddy Jake the Runaway and Short Stories
Told after Dark *(1889)*

Daddy Jake has a complexion different from Harris's earlier volumes of Remus tales. The six most interesting stories in the book
feature human protagonists, and Brer Rabbit has a role in only half
of the remaining tales. Indeed, one selection, "How the Birds
Talk," is not a story but a character sketch of Uncle Remus that is
followed by a delightful *tour de force* as he imitates the sounds that
owls and hens make when they carry on "conversations." The
frame of this character sketch primarily emphasizes Remus's vanity
and his dictatorial manner in the big house — except when he wants
extra food from the kitchen.

The most ambitious tale in the volume is "Daddy Jake, the Runaway," which is told in the third person. Set in 1863 on the Gaston
plantation in Putnam County, the three-part tale recounts the
attempts of little Lucien and Lillian Gaston to locate their favorite
companion, Daddy Jake, an old slave who had run off from the
plantation. As Harris explains, good overseers were hard to find in
1863; Jake had been wrongfully struck in the face by the foreman
recently hired on at the Gaston place; Jake had hit the man back
with an axe handle and had then fled into the canebrake along the
Oconee River. Harris builds some mild suspense into his tale when
the family goes looking for the absent children along the river. A
black woman, Crazy Sue, finds Lillian and Lucien asleep and
entertains them with a Brer Rabbit story before the plot is resolved:
the overseer had only been injured and had already been fired, and
Daddy Jake and the children find each other and return home
together. The whole family was happy, notes Harris, but "nobody
was any happier than Daddy Jake." Although Harris's story of
reconciliation and slave loyalty would appeal to an advocate of the
Old South, the portrait of Crazy Sue at least partly redeems the

tale. Years earlier her babies had died helplessly in a fire while she was being forced to work in a far-off field; overcome with grief, she had collapsed into the fire afterwards and had burned her face. She still thinks she can hear her babies crying; her distracted look at times, coupled with her physical disfiguration, had given her her name.

Ridding the landscape of demons is the theme of "How a Witch Was Caught" and of "Uncle Remus's Wonder Story." In the former tale, a preacher discovers that an evil cat that has been tormenting him is actually the miller's wife, who is secretly a witch and can transform her shape. The preacher and the miller realize that they must burn the woman, but fortunately for their sensibilities she reassumes the form of the cat before her execution. The story of the witch-wife is a traditional one, yet it is interesting to note Harris's subtle inversion of the exorcism theme in the tale's frame. Remus chastises the little boy for causing so much trouble and racket around the plantation by saying, " 'I knows deze yer white chillun, mon! ... Dey'll git de upper hand er de niggers ef de Lord spar's um. En he mos' inginner'lly spar's um.' "

The little boy often asked to hear "Uncle Remus's Wonder Story," which was reprinted in book form as *The Witch Wolf* in 1921. Uncle Remus's narrative style and his satiric emphases make this witch tale more humorous than horrifying, however. When the witch-wolf got hungry and wanted to eat a man, she had first to persuade him to marry her. She would change herself into a " 'likely young gal' " with the help of curling-irons, ribbons, and beau-catchers and would court the man assiduously — making sure to " 'nibble at 'er fan en fumble wid 'er hankcher.' " Luckily, her latest intended victim had become suspicious and had gone to Judge Rabbit for advice; as a result, he devised a test that proved she was a witch-wolf; and she immediately " 'made 'er disappearance in de elements.' "

Metamorphosis, a standard motif in supernatural tales, figures again, but more elaborately, in "The Little Boy and His Dogs." This tale is more frightening than the wonder story, and the social satire it contains is more pointed. The narrative combines two plot lines. A young boy, who is portrayed to be black, is searching for his kidnapped white-skinned sister when two well-dressed ladies come along asking for water, food, and directions. The boy and his mother oblige them, but the ladies follow the boy, who gets scared and climbs a tree. The ladies then shed their garments, revealing that they are really panthers underneath. Through various magical devices the boy escapes their clutches and calls in his dogs, which kill the panthers. Later he finds his sister, who has been made to work for an old bear. Using a Brer Rabbit strategy, the boy convinces the bear that he can curl his hair by putting his head into a pot of boiling water; the boy's dogs finish off the bear's cubs. The story also functions as a running racial satire. The boy wonders why "mighty fine ladies" would lap water like animals, eat bread voraciously with bared fangs, and be equipped with hairy hands and arms. At first his mother only assumes, "dat's de way de quality folks does, honey"; but, when the "quality" begin to pant like wild varmints and to run on all fours, the boy figures he had better climb the nearest tree. At the end of the panther episode, the boy's mother decides that she will never again set any store by folks with fine clothes. Allegorically, the tale also treats the familiar theme of the attempted dominance of weaker creatures by more rapacious ones. The young boy's devotion to his white sister suggests the value of love, rather than hatred, between the races.

V   Uncle Remus and His Friends: Old Plantation Stories, Songs, and Ballads with Sketches of Negro Character *(1892)*

Harris intended his fourth Uncle Remus volume — *Uncle Remus and His Friends* — to be his last, because he felt that the public was surely tiring of the fables after reading them for over a decade. Furthermore, Harris had become somewhat fatigued by the flurry of folkloristic commentary that his stories had generated. As he indicated in the prefatory notes to *Uncle Remus and His Friends,* he was now convinced that he knew even less about folklore than when he had published his first book. His seemingly learned introduction to *Nights with Uncle Remus* appeared in retrospect to be of "enterprising inconsequence," and he had concluded that almost nothing could be concluded about the origins and transmission of folklore. Harris also apologized for the thirty-four animal stories in *Uncle Remus and His Friends* as having been "caught for me in the kitchen" by household cooks and the Harris children, for Harris's reservoir of Putnam County tales and outlines from correspondents seems to have been running dry in the early 1890s. For several reasons, then, Harris announced that "the old man will bother the public no more with his whimsical stories." Yet, as I indicated in Chapter 2, Harris's readers were so delighted with *Uncle Remus and His Friends* that they soon demanded additional volumes; Uncle Remus would not be allowed to retire.

Harris made his "last" Remus book a compilation of several types of Old South writings. Its physical arrangement is similar to that of the first volume: the animal tales are followed by sixteen hymns, work songs, and ballads and by twenty-one sketches about Remus's experiences while he lived in Atlanta. Miss Sally and Mars John had moved after the Civil War to Atlanta where John has a law practice, and Remus still functions as a family retainer. In effect, then, Harris resurrects the Atlanta Remus from earlier *Constitution* days, and he supplies enough details to account for his character's removal from the Putnam plantation.

Several of the Atlanta sketches smack of Harris's own conservatism about new ideas, especially new-fangled inventions and contraptions; at the same time, however, old Uncle Remus unfortunately wears more vaudevillian greasepaint than realistic flesh tones. In "Uncle Remus at the Telephone," in "A Queer Experience with the Phonograph," and in "Uncle Remus on an Electric Car," for example, the old man is disconcerted and even superstitious when he is confronted by electrical machines that talk mysteriously and by streetcars that go " 'zoon.' " Remus becomes the complete minstrel darkey not only in the fifth sketch when a blind horse he had borrowed throws him through a honeysuckle vine and into a tree but also in "A Case of the Grippe," when he frightens off a delegation from the black Charity Burying Society by pretending to go into a trance and by jumping around the sick room on all fours.

Uncle Remus's Old South views on Negro education also suggest some of Harris's lingering racial prejudice. For example, in sketch XVIII Remus criticizes his daughter for sending her son to school. Young William Henry had only been taught how to get into trouble at school, Remus observes, and his attempts at holding down a regular job always ended unhappily. Remus chastises William Henry for his irresponsibility and claims that he is destined for the chain-gang. " 'Wid me,' " Remus states as conservatively as he had in the 1870s, " 'a nigger is done gradjywated de minnit you puts de plough handles in his han's.' " From one perspective, Remus himself comes across as something of a shirker in the seventh sketch, when he avoids cutting down the weeds in Miss Sally's backyard by asking her if she has seen the snake yet; from another point of view, however, Remus is only indulging in some of

Brer Rabbit's trickery around the other "creeturs."

The most accomplished of the plantation animal stories in the *Friends* volume are again trickster tales that feature Brer Rabbit. But the boy is older now and more skeptical, and Remus has become more resigned to the fact that his listener will require fuller explanations of the marvelous events in the animal kingdom that he has formerly passed along as fact and with minimal comment or documentation. Thus several of the story-frames in Harris's fourth book include Remus's disclaimers: he is only retelling stories that he has heard from others, and explanations about improbable occurrences are simply not available. Also, the old man takes more time now to remark about the similarities and differences between animal and human behavior or "morality."

In tale XVIII, for instance, Remus responds to the boy's observation (which the youth had heard from his father) that animals do not have " 'sure enough sense' " by rehearsing some of the intelligent feats that animals can do: the blue cow knows when to shake the plum tree and get corn out of the crib, and the brindle cow has learned how to open all the plantation gates with her horn. " 'Take um up one side en down de yuther, en all 'roun' ez fur ez dey go,' " says Remus, and the creatures " 'got much sense ez folks. Dey ain't got law sense, en dey ain't got buyin' en sellin' sense, but what dey want wid it? What dey gwine do wid it ef dey had it?' " The animals know how to do what they need to do, generalizes the old man; they " 'done got der eddycation,' " and if the smaller creatures have more sense, " 'dey bleedz ter have it.' " Brer Rabbit is full of tricks, but " 'What folks calls tricks is creetur sense.' "

Brer Rabbit's " 'creetur sense' " and his unfettered mischievousness lead him, in the eighth tale, into tempting Brer Fox with some chicken gizzards if the fox will help him carry a load of hay. When Brer Rabbit sets the hay on fire and burns the fox's back, the little boy protests the cruelty of his actions. Remus only responds that " 'You might talk dat away 'bout folks, but creeturs — well, folks is folks en creeturs is creeturs, en you can't make um needer mo' ner less.' " " 'You er what you is, en you can't be no is-er,' " Remus continues in the next tale. " 'I'm what I am en I can't be no am-er. It all done been fix' " (Harris may have been thinking of his own "fixed" personality when he wrote this). To prove his point, Remus follows Brer Rabbit's hay-burning prank with a tale about another more insidious trick. The rabbit has the gall to give Brer

Fox a salve secretly laced with red pepper to help him soothe his blistered back; the salve produces another screech of pain; and Brer Rabbit apologizes for having accidentally handed him the wrong ointment.

Lacking other motivation, then, Brer Rabbit's own compulsiveness as a trickster constantly stirs him up to find additional, and even more insulting, tricks to pull on the stronger animals. As Robert Bone contends, Brer Rabbit lives in a world of assault, beatings, and tortures in which the law of the jungle prevails; and resistance and subversion, not submission or accommodation, are basic to survival. Since Brer Rabbit, the cagey and aggressive folk hero of the Negro slave, was reared in a brier patch, "he is one tough bunny."[33] As wily as his hero, old Uncle Remus conveys through the symbolical and allegorical texture of his tales the black man's perspective, one conditioned by two centuries of suffering and toil. The white man is what he is and " 'can't be no is-er,' " and therefore the Negro was " 'bleedz' " to have " 'creetur sense' " and to play his "tricks."

CHAPTER 4

Later Uncle Remus Tales, and Stories for Children

I The Tar-Baby and Other Rhymes of Uncle Remus *(1904)*

HARRIS continued to publish magazine pieces after his retirement from the *Constitution* in 1900, and unabated public enthusiasm for Uncle Remus, plus his own love of poetry and delight with the rhythms of language and folk song, led him to write a series of versified Uncle Remus stories for the *Saturday Evening Post.* Collected as a book and handsomely illustrated in sepia tones in 1904, *The Tar-Baby and Other Rhymes of Uncle Remus* gathers rhymed versions of nine Remus-type stories, as well as seventeen lyrics, songs, and hymns. As Harris pointed out in an introductory note, all but two of the rhymed tales were new; of the hymns and songs, ten had previously been published in *Uncle Remus.* Harris apologized with tongue in cheek for Remus's versifying by explaining that the old man used an iambic four-beat line as "the simplest form of narrative verse," for Remus had no notion of the "science of English verse" and of the "misleading rules of the professors of prosody."

Harris also included in his introduction the disconcerting observation, which folklorists have apparently overlooked, that the tar-baby tale had been "thrown into a rhymed form for the purpose of presenting and preserving what seems to be the genuine version." Although Harris was perhaps alluding to a rhythmic style of narrative delivery, one with rising and falling intonation patterns, a representative passage from the tar-baby story-poem is more heavily rhymed than we might expect that a plantation narrative, recited in the slave quarters, would have been:

> Brer Rabbit, he skipped along at las' —
> He skip sorter slow, den he skip kinder fas' —
> Kaze he use de spring ez a lookin'-glass,
> An' he seed de Tar-Baby settin' dar:
> "Good-mornin', suh, an' how's yo' Ma?
> An' how does yo' copperositee
> Seem ter segashuate?" sezee;
> "An' whar yo' manners? You mus be deff!
> You'll hear ef I hit you, an' you'll lose yo' breff!"

Of the new material, the most delightful poem is Remus's humorous account of the Fall of Man in "De Appile-Tree," for Remus notes that Adam and Eve

> had der frolics an' dey had der flings,
> An' den atter dat der fun tuck wings.
> Honey mighty sweet, but bees got stings.

The problem for modern man, of course, is that the apple-tree scattered her seeds "bofe fur an' free, / An' dat's what de matter wid you an' me." The old man continues:

> Talk about troubles! I got um an' had um,
> An' I know mighty well dat I cotch um fum Adam.

There is no doubt a good deal of Harris himself in Remus's more lyrical poems, "It's Good to be Old if You Know How to Do" and "Uncle Remus Captures a Dream." In the first poem, Remus explains that his advanced age has led to a new understanding of death, the mutability of things, and the importance of personal memories. The second poem is an intriguing piece of dream-psychology in which Remus talks about the strange interrelationship in dreams of real experience, memories, and wishes.

Although "Baylor's Mail" appears to describe only a hurried journey across the Southern terrain, Harris explained this song's folkloristic value in an accompanying note. He wrote that Negroes on Southern plantations had developed a system of hollers and hand-signals for communicating messages with surprising speed. When Sherman left Atlanta, for example, all the Negroes and one white person (young Joe Harris) on one Middle Georgia plantation knew of his departure within twelve hours. A similar hollering technique was used in India and Africa, Harris observed, and he believed that the African prince Qua had introduced this form of communication on Southern plantations around 1800. Qua had a grandson named M'Bulu, and the older Negroes called the message system M'Bulu Irruwandu, or M'Bulu's breech clout. Through corruption of the language, the message-conveying technique came to be called Baylor's Mail.

II   Told by Uncle Remus: New Stories of the Old Plantation *(1905)*

More than twelve years after he thought he had published his last Uncle Remus tale in *Uncle Remus and His Friends* (1892), Harris made his final major compilation of folk stories, *Told by Uncle Remus,* which functions both sociologically and esthetically as an epilogue to the Remus cycle of tales and to the old plantation era. In his sensitively written prefatory sketch, entitled "The Reason Why," Harris explained that Remus had some years earlier moved with Miss Sally and her family to Atlanta and had retired from storytelling when the little boy grew up and married. But Uncle Remus had soon become restless and unhappy with the " 'dust, an' mud, an' money' " of postwar Atlanta and had told Sally that he wished to return to the old farm in Putnam County. He was delighted to learn that Sally and John were going back, also, now that their son was married. When the son of the former "little boy" visited the plantation, Remus came out of his retirement to tell him some old stories — the fifteen tales in the volume.

"The Reason Why" is a complex piece. Not only does it reveal Harris's own ambivalency about the impatient and money-oriented New South as compared to the peaceful and pastoral times before the war, but it also provides a critique of new notions about child-rearing and comments in poignant terms about the problems of old age. The son of the little boy is a frail and somewhat feminine youth who had undergone too much disciplining by his Atlanta-born mother; as a result, he does not display enough boyishness, mischievousness, and imagination to Remus's and Grandmother Sally's way of thinking. The pale little child talks properly and precisely, like a much older youth; and, furthermore, he seems to lack a sense of humor. Harris speaks for both Uncle Remus and Sally when he observes that "The trouble with the boy was that he had had no childhood; he had been subdued and weakened by the abnormal training he had received." Remus sets about humanizing the "unduly repressed" child, and *Told by Uncle Remus* is in effect a continuous narrative of encounter between the man and the boy. By the end of the volume the young lad has made considerable progress toward being a real boy; in fact, once or twice Remus even has to temper the child's newly discovered willfulness and independence.

Allying themselves against the boy's mother in their efforts to introduce a little vigor into the lad's system helps bring Remus and Sally closer together, but primarily it is their mutual old age that seems to break down the barriers between black and white, and between lower and higher social station. Remus and Sally share a quiet sympathy; the two talk of feeling useless, and at times a gesture or a glance is sufficient to express their sense of helplessness. In his mutually reflecting portraits of Sally and Uncle Remus, Harris is also suggesting that survivors of the Old South, those remaining patrons of former times, can only turn to each other for support and understanding; for the new postwar generation has a different system of values and a different cultural and social orientation.

Reminiscent of his method in *Nights with Uncle Remus,* Harris frames the stories in the *Told* volume with considerable care and effect. In the framing that surrounds "Why Mr. Cricket has Elbows on his Legs," for instance, we discover that Sally is irritable because the boy's mother had confined him to the parlor for a minor offense (wiping his sticky mouth on his coatsleeve), but that Sally is hesitant to criticize the woman for her severity lest her own identity as "Grandmother" become replaced by the less attractive one of "mother-in-law." Remus entertains the boy with anecdotes about his father, who would have made the parlor look as if a hurricane had struck if he had ever been locked up in it. Remus also makes pointed comments within earshot of the boy's mother about how a young lad made a parlor-prisoner for no discernible offense would grow up rebellious and find himself in a sure-enough jail later on. The mother relents and turns her son out to play, and Remus tells him a story.

As the days go by, Remus works to expand the scope of the boy's imagination and to educate him out of his literal-mindedness. Discovering that the lad was picturing a real locale like Atlanta when Remus mentioned Brer Rabbit's laughing-place, the old man tells his new companion the story of how Brer Rabbit tricked the creatures into believing he actually had a secret laughing-place. When the creatures agree that Brer Fox can see the place first, Brer Rabbit makes him plunge through a thicket and into a hornet's nest; the rabbit laughs heartily as the fox rolls on the ground and runs in circles snapping at the stinging insects. When Brer Fox protests later that he did not see anything funny about the so-called laughing-place, Brer Rabbit responds, "I said 'twuz my laughin'-place, an' I'll say it ag'in."

In the frame of the next tale, "Brother Rabbit and the Chickens," the little boy tells Remus a story that he likes — "Cinderella" — and complains that the animals in the old man's tales lied and were cruel to each other. Remus counters with the analogy that " 'de creeturs ain't much ahead of folks.' " Furthermore, the animals even have an advantage over people because the creatures live according to their instincts and do not concern themselves with right and wrong; folks, however, have to turn to their preachers to find out when they are going astray. Remus's observation anticipates some of Twain's sardonic comments about the Moral Sense and about human and animal behavior in "The Mysterious Stranger," published eleven years later; but Remus's statements also subtly reflect the black man's experience with the inhumanities of chattel slavery. The creatures " 'hatter scuffle an' scramble an' git 'long de bes' way dey kin,' " says Remus, implying that the Negro's code of survival obliged him to shiftiness and trickery in the face of superior force.

Remus then tells a story to illustrate these themes. Brer Rabbit easily rationalizes stealing chickens from Mr. Man (if the man wanted his chickens back, he could always ask for them); and, after eating them, he realizes that he now has to dispose of the feathers. When he puts them in a bag and convinces Brer Fox that they are a special kind of grass, worth nine dollars a pound, that rich folks grind up to make Whipmewhopme pudding, Brer Fox quickly volunteers to carry the bag to the mill for a small fee. When Mr. Man spots the feathers sticking out of the sack, he " 'whips and whops' " the fox for stealing his chickens while Brer Rabbit laughs at the scene from the bushes. In the closing frame of the story, the boy says that he cannot see why the rabbit thought the scene was so funny. Remus looks hard at this "modern little boy," a product of New South meliorism, and replies that the boy did not know Brer Fox very well. " 'I don't speck you hear talk er de way he try ter git de inturn on Brer Rabbit,' " he observes in an oblique reference to the condition of things in " 'dem days,' " before the Civil War. As to the rabbit's enjoyment of the scene, Remus only admits pithily and ironically that it " 'sholy wuz scan'lous de way Brer Rabbit kin laugh.' "

As in previous tales, Uncle Remus enjoys his own brand of tricks and power-plays around white folks. When he sees that the health of his young friend from the city has improved during his plantation stay, and that the boy is now progressing admirably in the art of mischief-making, Remus feels the time is ripe for a Brer Rabbit–style trick to remind the white lad of his mortality. One afternoon while Remus is half-dozing in the sun, he spies the boy stealing up on him. The old man feigns sleep; and, just as the lad is about to jump at him, he suddenly straightens himself in his chair and gives out a blood-curdling yell. The boy is almost paralyzed with fright, and it takes him a moment or so to get his breath. With typical indirection, Remus pretends ignorance and thanks the boy for awakening him in the middle of a horrifying dream that he had been having about going to the bad place on a runaway train.

This episode works subtly but effectively as the introductory framework for "When Brother Rabbit was King," which is a study in the reversal of roles and a satire on royal "benevolence." The king of the land had grown tired of kinging and wanted a vacation, Remus explains, and he agreed to pay Brer Rabbit a dollar a day to take his place. Thus Brer Rabbit " 'done de kingin' whiles de King gone a-fishin'.' " Before long the rabbit discovers that the king's servants in effect do the kinging for him, so he relaxes until an urgent case is finally brought to his attention. It seems that Mr. Dog felt that he and his " 'kinnery' " were not being treated properly, for they now found bones where they used to find meat. Brer Rabbit, recognizing Mr. Dog as the same creature who had chased him so often, adjusts his crown and orders the dog rubbed with turpentine and red pepper and run out of the palace. When his " 'kinnery' " come looking for their envoy, they are told that Mr. Dog had indeed come by to " 'po' mouf' " and that he had been given " 'all dat a gen'termun dog could ax fer.' " To this day, Remus closes in etiological fashion, one can see dogs sniffing bushes and stumps and growling, looking for the kinsman who betrayed their cause. As social allegory, Remus's ironic story satirizes the ineffectuality, and the brutality, of the feudal system of Old South slavery that was claimed by its adherents to be both humane and just.

III   Uncle Remus and Brer Rabbit *(1907),* Uncle Remus
and the Little Boy *(1910), and Later Volumes*

Of the two small collections of Remus tales appearing around the
time of Harris's death, *Uncle Remus and Brer Rabbit* is of interest
because the six tales and the five poems in the volume are illustrated
with large, multicolored cartoons, two for each page of text. As I
have indicated. J. M. Condé's carefully detailed pictures are fore-
runners of the newspaper and movie cartoons that have become
permanent features in American popular culture. The tales in the
collection display the rabbit in his usual role as trickster. *Uncle
Remus and the Little Boy* contains five poems, a song, and seven
stories that continue the narrative cycle in which Remus educates
his young listener about animal and human behavior. One of these
tales, the etiological "Brer Rabbit Has Trouble with the Moon"
has parallels with a Játaka story of India in which a hare fights with
the moon. The creatures lived near Unk Moon in the days before
the moon became angry with Brer Rabbit for being saucy, hit him
in the mouth, and split his lip. Brer Rabbit, who fought back, left
Unk Moon with a scarred face; and all the creatures then took a
long jump and settled permanently on earth.

Uncle Remus and the Little Boy also brings to an official conclusion the Remus–little boy relationship. In "Uncle Remus Receives a
Letter," old Mars John reads Remus a delightful epistle — one
replete with misspellings and unconscious humor — that had been
penned by the old master's grandson. This letter recounts the second little boy's train ride to Atlanta after his plantation visit and
reveals how much he is enjoying his newly discovered mischievousness. Then the reader learns in the frame of the sixth tale that the
young lad has just returned from a trip to southern California for
his health and that he is now feeling quite vigorous indeed. The
series of encounters between the old man and his latest friend, who
now appears to have fully acquired his long-overdue boyishness,
could properly be said to end here.

After Harris's death, his daughter-in-law Julia, who searched
newspaper and periodical files, published five Atlanta Remus
sketches and six animal tales in *Uncle Remus Returns* (1918). She
believed that Harris would have included these in a sequel to *Told
by Uncle Remus* had his editorial duties for *Uncle Remus's Magazine* not consumed so much of his energy. In these Atlanta
sketches, which are similar to those discussed earlier, Remus com-

plains about recalcitrant mules, hypocritical church activities, and
" 'sunshine niggers' " that are afraid of work. As in *Told by Uncle
Remus,* the animal fables are framed with comments about the
little boy's sheltered life and with accounts of his walks and conversations with the old storyteller. The most suggestive of the folk
tales is the fourth narrative in which Brer Rabbit's ability to read
enables him to con Brer Fox and his wife out of two pullets. In this
story, the weaker race ironically proves to have the higher educa-
tional level.

Thomas English's edition of seven uncollected Remus tales, published in 1948,[1] is the last one of original Harris stories. Five of the
tales had been published from 1889 to 1892 in *Dixie,* an Atlanta
publication, and the other two were found in manuscript among
the papers in the Harris Collection at Emory University. As English
points out in his introduction, four of the *Dixie* pieces and one of
the manuscript tales were revised to delete the Negro dialect and
were published in *Little Mr. Thimblefinger and His Queer Country*
(1894) and in its sequel, *Mr. Rabbit at Home* (1895). Harris apparently had doubts about the authenticity of the stories as black folklore and was therefore hesitant about including them in another
Remus volume. Harris may, however, have been overly cautious
with three of his stories; for, as English notes, the brief "Mr.
Goat's Short Tail" and "The Baby and the Punkins," which are
printed under the title "Two Little Tales as Told by Old Uncle
Remus," are derivative of Jamaican Negro folklore and are probably as worthy of inclusion as Daddy Jack's Gullah stories in
Nights with Uncle Remus. Similarly, "Brother Rabbit Doesn't Go
to See Aunt Nancy" features a spider-witch, Aunt Nancy, who is
the equivalent of Annancy, the Jamaican folk hero. Of the remaining four stories in the collection, two are etiological tales that
account for the buzzard's inability to sing and for the bear's prowess as a wrestler, and two others feature Brer Rabbit in the predictable role of trickster.

IV   *Books for Children*

Harris observed to an interviewer late in his life that he wrote
stories for children because he liked young people but "not in the
usual way, with a kiss or a hug." Rather, "I get down to their level,
think with them and play with them. I was a child in feeling when I
began to write for other children, and haven't grown up yet."[2]

Although Harris was even too self-conscious to tell his stories to his own children, he sought to communicate with youngsters and to show his sensitivity to their needs in his writings. Viewed from one perspective, the Uncle Remus volumes are stories for children; but, as we have seen, their humor, folkloristic value, and psychological and sociological complexities have given them considerable stature among adult readers of all critical persuasions. During the 1890s, however, Harris wrote five volumes of tales primarily for the young; and he added a sixth book in 1903. *Little Mr. Thimblefinger and His Queer Country* (1894), *Mr. Rabbit at Home* (1895), *The Story of Aaron* (1895), *Aaron in the Wildwoods* (1897), *Plantation Pageants* (1899), and *Wally Wanderoon and His Story-Telling Machine* (1903) are set on a Middle Georgia plantation before or during the war; and each is attractively illustrated.

Except for *Aaron in the Wildwoods,* all of these books recount the adventures of seven-year-old Sweetest Susan; eight-year-old Buster John; and their crotchety but loyal Negro nursemaid, Drusilla. In the first two volumes, the children's adventures take place in a magical kingdom below the plantation spring. The techniques the children use to gain entry to the kingdom, as well as the eccentric but delightful inhabitants they meet there — including reverse images of themselves who live in a looking-glass — suggest Lewis Carroll's vision in *Alice's Adventures in Wonderland* (1865) and *Through the Looking-Glass* (1872). Harris claimed, however, never to have read the Alice books, although he knew about Carroll's works.[3]

The bulk of the six volumes consists of folk stories that are told to the children by various narrators, but these narratives include semiautobiographical episodes based upon Harris's own youthful experiences on the Turner plantation during the War. Harris's brief introductory note to *Little Mr. Thimblefinger* comments, in effect, about all six of his children's books. Some of the stories "were gathered from the negroes, but were not embodied in the tales of Uncle Remus, because I was not sure they were negro stories; some are Middle Georgia folklore stories, and no doubt belong to England; and some are merely inventions." In an aside to the reader at the end of the fifth volume in the series, Harris reflects the unusual looseness of his tales in the children's books: he apologizes for his work as a "patchwork of memories and fancies, a confused dream of old times." The books vary considerably in artistic merit. The first two volumes can be considered together since *Mr.*

Rabbit at Home was written as a sequel to *Little Mr. Thimblefinger and His Queer Country.* Tiny Mr. Thimblefinger and his friend the Grandmother of the Dolls visit the nursery one night when the children and Drusilla happen to be awake. Mr. Thimblefinger subsequently invites them to join him under the spring, which they can do only if they enter the water at nine minutes and nine seconds after twelve noon — at that time alone the water is not wet. Drusilla, who is skeptical about the proposed adventure, warns Sweetest Susan and Buster John, " 'Ef you gits drownded in dar I'll sho' tell yo' ma.' " But she surrenders at the last second and accompanies the children to Mr. Thimblefinger's strange world, where everyone can jump higher and farther than normal and where, among other surprising inhabitants, reside giant Mr. Rabbit and Miss Meadows, now grown old and gray.

Harris uses Mr. Rabbit and Miss Meadows primarily as storytellers, but Mr. Thimblefinger and other residents of the underwater world also contribute tales for the children's entertainment. Many of the stories in the two volumes are of European origin; the tales of the witch of the well, the magic ring, and the bewitched huntsman parallel traditional Continental fairy tales. Harris doubtless drew upon these tales because their protagonists are frequently young girls or boys. Etiological stories of the Uncle Remus variety and tales about Brer Rabbit comprise the rest.

Harris's most accomplished writing in the first two books is his treatment of Drusilla and the other figures as they interact between storytelling sessions or interrupt tales to comment about them. For example, in "Mr. Rabbit as a Rain-Maker," Mr. Rabbit tells how he conned all the animals into bringing him food in return for rain during a long drought; when the creatures squalled and fought and could not decide how much rain they actually wanted, Mr. Rabbit took the food as pay for their folly. Mr. Thimblefinger's interjection at this point, which smacks of Mark Twain's style of humor, rounds off the tale perfectly: " 'If there had been many more such fools in your neighborhood...you could have set up a grocery-store.' " Thimblefinger's enjoyment of Mr. Rabbit's stories is not reciprocated; for the rabbit, who becomes irritated because none of Thimblefinger's tales has any discernible moral, is found dozing before long whenever the little man begins a new narrative. He occasionally rouses himself to make a sardonic comment, as he does at the end of a long and complicated tale about a shoemaker's two sons and the king's daughter. That story beats anything he ever heard, says the rabbit, " 'for *length*.' " Drusilla's cantankerous remarks and asides occasionally have a social barb embedded in them, for she is weary of " 'playin' nuss' " to mischievous white girls and boys and " 'gwine in all kind er quare places whar you dunner when ner whar you kin git out.' " She interjects her most apt comment at the beginning of a tale about a scary, green-goggled Woog that lives on the other side of the looking-glass. Drusilla hopes that the Woog stays on his side of the glass, because " 'Black folks don't stan' much chance wid dem what knows 'em, let 'lone dem ar Woog an' things what don't know 'em.' "

In *The Story of Aaron,* Buster John, Sweetest Susan, and Drusilla hear a series of narratives about the adventures of Aaron, a slave who is a full-blooded Arab and the foreman of the field hands on the Abercrombie plantation. The children and their nursemaid do not appear at all in *Aaron in the Wildwoods,* which is set some fifteen years earlier and which recounts Aaron's experiences with Little Crotchet, a crippled child who later died and whom the children refer to in *The Story of Aaron* as their deceased uncle.

Aaron, who is one of the few overtly "romantic" figures in the Harris canon, has piercing black eyes, thin lips, brown skin, and wavy black hair; and the Negroes on the Abercrombie plantation, who think Aaron is a conjurer, testify to his powers over men and animals. As Harris explains, Aaron was the son of Ben Ali, an Arab slave trader who, ironically, had himself been captured and sold into slavery by a powerful African tribe. Ben Ali had subsequently managed to marry another Arabian captive, and Aaron was their only child. Once Aaron has taught the children how to talk to his animal friends, the animals themselves — the black stallion Timoleon, the gray pony Gristle, the track dog Rambler, and the white pig Grunter — share in telling how Aaron came to be the plantation overseer. Aaron had wanted to work for the Abercrombies, but cruel and uncouth Mr. Gossett had tricked young Master Abercrombie at the auction block and had himself purchased Aaron to work on his small farm. After a fight with Gossett's son, Aaron hid in the swamp, eluded the Gossett's "nigger dogs," and was secretly aided by Little Crotchet. In a touch that foreshadows the Snopses' tactics in Faulkner's novels, the resentful poor-white Gossetts burned down the Abercrombie place, although no one could prove they did it. Aaron heroically saved Little Crotchet, and only then did the selfish Gossetts relent somewhat and sell the Arab to the boy's family.

As was the case with "Daddy Jake, the Runaway," Harris's story ends too easily; for Aaron happily resumes his role as slave, although serving under a more humane master this time. The conclusion of *The Story of Aaron* thus seems to belie Aaron's romantic individualism and his supernatural powers. However, *Aaron in the Wildwoods* is a more esthetically satisfying book because, although Harris essentially retells the Arab's story, he does so from a consistent third-person point of view. He also elaborates details of plot, and he provides more thorough portraits of the Gossetts and a more psychologically compelling atmosphere of suspense. The second volume in no way tarnishes, however, the Old South image of Aaron's contentment and loyalty as the Abercrombies' slave foreman.

Harris's sentimentalized portrait of Little Crotchet, especially the closing death-bed scene, his personification of the swamp at night, and his humorous account of the Gossetts' frustrated search for their runaway would appeal to younger readers. But, for the mature reader, Harris's editorializing in the eighth chapter about the benefits of slavery is disturbingly racist. Although his apologetic view was probably intended to simplify a complex problem for his more youthful readers, he nevertheless revealed a continuing belief that the white man's burden was to rescue black children from their primeval darkness. With American slavery happily a thing of the past, writes Harris, and the tumult and bloodshed of the Civil War over, Americans can see that slavery "redeemed" the Negro from a worse bondage in Africa — one of ignorance and savagery. The hand of "an All-wise Providence" had helped to bring the Negro into "close and stimulating contact with Christian civilization" and to lift him up to the benefits and blessings of citizenship in only two hundred years — a more rapid rise than any other branch of the human race had known. Slavery was bondage, but it was also a type of "university"; and the price America paid for such education was small when it considers the ultimate benefits of freedom and citizenship for the Negro.

The last of Harris's books for children, *Plantation Pageants* and *Wally Wanderoon and His Story-Telling Machine,* also form a two-part narrative sequence. As *The Story of Aaron* drew to a close, Harris portrayed Susan's and Buster John's sense of wonder when they saw Sherman's army march by the Abercrombie plantation on its way to the sea; Harris had also described the army's passing in his autobiographical narrative *On the Plantation. Plantation*

Pageants and *Wally Wanderoon* recount the children's adventures just after Sherman's appearance and continue to draw upon Harris's recollections of his days at Turner's plantation. As had been the situation at Turnwold, Sherman's men did little damage to the Abercrombie farm; in fact, the soldiers even restored the cattle and protected the buildings from harm. Harris carefully controls his imagery in describing the atmosphere at the Abercrombie place after the troops had finally left: the plantation seemed different, silent and depressing; an east wind blew, and the animals were jittery. As the days passed, most of the Negroes who had left the plantation " 'huntin' freedom' " drifted back; they did not like what they had seen of freedom and realized that it might mean even more work than they had known at the Abercrombies'. Around the plantation, notes Harris with some sensitivity, the returned Negroes talked and moved quietly; they were "not sure of their position" and, ironically, "freedom appeared to add to their shyness."

Wally Wanderoon is the last in Harris's gallery of storytellers for children, and Harris introduces him with an appropriate Old South touch: aged Mr. Wanderoon is poking around the road in search of the "Good Old Times." Since Wally likes traditional stories that begin "Once upon a time...," he is irritated whenever the little narrator inside his old-fashioned storytelling machine interrupts himself to explain or to footnote a tale's "scientific" aspects. Using a technique from the Mr. Thimblefinger books, Harris humorously depicts the banter and the badinage among the several characters as they argue about their favorite types of tales. In this volume Drusilla finally relents and enters into the spirit of things by telling four of her favorite stories. Appropriately, one is a Brer Rabbit tale; another, an etiological story which includes an explanation of why the Negro is black; and two depict romantic marriages between lovers from different social classes.

The final volume in Harris's series of childrens' books closes with subtle rhetorical effect. Wally Wanderoon disappears from view while he is still looking for the Old Times, and the children and Drusilla are suddenly back in the real world again. They wonder whether it was all a dream, but how could they all dream the same dream? The child's imagination often projects a dream-world, suggests Harris; the Old Times, the Old South are now only a dream, but those who so wish can still share in it.

CHAPTER 5

The Short Fiction

I *The Critical Reception of the Short Stories*

WHEN *Mingo and Other Sketches in Black and White* appeared in 1884, reviewers were delighted to discover that Harris could write effective local-color and realistic works. But Harris remained so completely identified with his extremely popular Uncle Remus tales that reminders by the critics of his "other mode" continued regularly into the middle of the twentieth century. By the 1960s, when "Free Joe and the Rest of the World" or "Aunt Fountain's Prisoner" began to be included in anthologies of American literature along with "The Wonderful Tar-Baby Story" and "The Moon in the Mill-Pond," Harris's reputation as a local colorist was firmly established.

Typical of the early critics' responses to Harris's short stories are those of James C. Derby and William Baskervill. Both men admired Harris's portraits of the Southern poor white and the mountaineer, and they praised his ability to represent other phases of Negro character besides those shown in the Uncle Remus volumes.[1] In 1903 Horace S. Fiske recalled how enthusiastically Harris's stories of "low life" had been received when they were first published, and he emphasized their subtle humor, dramatic power, and strongly individualized characters.[2]

F. P. Gaines and John Herbert Nelson commended Harris for his realism in his portraits of Free Joe, Mingo, and other postwar characters; and Gaines saw these figures as redeeming their author somewhat from the sentimentality and romanticism in the portrait of Uncle Remus.[3] Sterling Brown, however, argued that Mingo, Aunt Fountain, and Balaam, along with Remus, remained stereotypes that represented orthodox Southern attitudes about the Negro's social position. Brown did observe that in "Where's Duncan?" and "Free Joe" Harris had disclosed some of the uglier aspects of slavery.[4] Darwin Turner agreed substantially with Brown that Harris's Negro characters, whether slave or free, still largely projected the white man's behavioral ideals for the black man.[5]

Jay B. Hubbell, Claude Simpson, and Wade Hall have praised Harris's skill as a local colorist. Harris, who called himself a "Georgia cracker," spoke the language of the people; and he wrote sensitively about the changing social and economic values in the South during Reconstruction. Hall, who gave special attention to the Civil War tales, indicated that they showed Harris's sense of the absurdity of war and emphasized the need for reconciliation between North and South.[6] But the fullest discussions of Harris's short fiction are found in Shields McIlwaine's lively and sensitive *The Southern Poor-White from Lubberland to Tobacco Road*[7] and in Merrill Maguire Skaggs's comprehensive *The Folk of Southern Fiction*.[8] McIlwaine acknowledges that Harris's love for the plain people, his avoidance of sex and the sordid, and his propagandizing for North-South reconciliation often led to sentimentality, strained pathos, and facile endings in stories that might have been more complex; nevertheless, he created a handful of truly memorable Southern poor-white characters. Skaggs points out that Harris was virtually the only local colorist to portray the poor white and that he succeeded in humanizing the stereotype of the "white trash" that existed in the popular mind. Many of Harris's local-color tales are gently satiric, which raises them above the level of mere sentimentality; and Harris recognizes in stories like "Little Compton" and *At Teague Poteet's* the Southern penchant for violent resolutions of disagreements.

Echoing the perspectives of most of Harris's informed critics, Skaggs concludes that Harris stresses throughout his short stories the virtues of respect, forgiveness, understanding, and love among human beings from all walks of life and from all political persuasions. As was the case in the narrative frames of the Uncle Remus tales and the children's stories, as well as in Harris's newspaper and periodical essays, the need for acceptance and reconciliation among America's "peoples" is the obvious theme in the short fiction. Yet, beneath the surface, we see revealed Harris's sensitivity as an author, and his conscious or unconscious need to confront his own private history in his writing.

II   Mingo and Other Sketches in Black and White *(1884)*

In 1884 Harris observed in a letter to the editor of *Current* that "no novel or story can be genuinely American, unless it deals with the *common people, that is, country people.*"[9] In a subsequent article on "The American Type" for *Current,* Harris also noted that because American novelists and storytellers too often treat only the comic aspects of provincial life, E. W. Howes's *The Story of a Country Town* (1883) deserves special praise because it reveals the tragic side of rural life. Had Harris used the adjective "poignant" or "realistic" instead of "tragic," he would have been describing the tone of several of his own local-color stories about country life.

"Mingo: A Sketch of Life in Middle Georgia" is a psychological study of two kinds of Southern consciousness. Mrs. Feratia Bivins is a poor white whose pride in self and family never recovered from the snubbing she received from an aristocratic lady. Mingo, a former slave, who had become Mrs. Bivins's helper on her small Putnam County farm after the Civil War, is one of Harris's most sensitive portraits of the black man; he is an especially fine study because his perceptions of human nature are more complete than those of the whites around him.

Harris opens the tale with a subtle symbolical touch that reveals Mingo's higher level of awareness. The first-person narrator, who is essentially a Harris-figure, has returned after a sixteen-year absence to Crooked Creek Church, which he had attended as a boy; and he is a little dismayed to find that the parishioners have aged so much and so visibly reflect the anxiety and uncertainty of "the period of desolation and disaster through which they had passed."[10] Even the church itself seems somehow smaller and darker than it used to be; and, as the narrator glances around the sanctuary for something that would link him to the past, he is disconcerted to find that the minister, now white-haired and enfeebled, no longer recognizes him. Then across the chamber he sees Mingo, who was formerly Judge Junius Wornum's carriage-driver. Although his face, too, shows the settled anxiety of the postwar years, the old black man looks as strong and erect as he had in his younger days when he was known as "Laughing Mingo" and had led the Rockville youths on wild escapades. Furthermore, unlike the white minister, Mingo immediately recognizes the narrator and smiles and gestures in salutation with a graceful motion of his hand. Not only has Mingo proven more physically resilient than the whites in the community, implies Harris, but his mental faculties have also remained keener. Harris's portrait of Mingo is an intriguing anticipation of Faulkner's studies in black endurance and strength of character.

After the Sunday service, Mingo moves confidently and familiarly through the crowd of whites and blacks to invite the narrator to join " 'Miss F'raishy' " and her granddaughter for a basketlunch on the grass. Feratia Bivins, tall and angular in her old age but as decisive and opinionated as she had ever been, had also recognized the narrator; but it becomes apparent before long that her invitation to lunch stems largely from ulterior motives. Feratia is glad to have a captive audience before whom she can rehearse the story of her family's suffering because of Mrs. Emily Wornum's false pride of station. Yet Feratia's recital of wrongs is doubly ironic: it reveals her own false pride of station, and it also seems to be her unconscious attempt to assuage her sense of guilt at having in time caused Mrs. Wornum to suffer.

Feratia's story, which occupies the second part of the tale, is another of Harris's delightful yet always precise pieces of dialect-writing. The old lady, who talks incessantly, shifts from one pet peeve to another — " ' new issue' " social-climbers; hospitality, which only the folks of her class understand; and no-count Negroes. But she gradually focuses upon her real subject: the marriage of aristocratic Judge and Emily Wornum's daughter Cordelia to her own son, Henry Clay Bivins. Of course, Feratia believed that her son was a fine match for Deely, despite his poor-white origins; but the Wornums felt otherwise. " '. . . if you'd 'a' heern the rippit them Wornums kicked up,' " observes Mrs. Bivins defiantly, " 'you'd 'a' thought the pore chile'd done took 'n' run off 'long of a whole passel er high pirates frum somewheres er 'nother.' " After the marriage, Judge Wornum seemed to go out of his head; and Emily Wornum cut her daughter off and forbade the Wornum Negroes to visit her. Mingo and the other Wornum blacks came to see Deely, anyhow, a fact which elicits from Feratia a condescending note of praise: " 'Niggers is niggers, but them Wornum niggers was a cut er two 'bove the common run.' " The narrator points out that, in complimenting the Wornum Negroes, Mrs. Bivins was "in no wise compromising her own dignity"; for, as Skaggs observes, Feratia's instinctively antagonistic attitude toward Negroes is typically that of the poor white toward the black.[11]

When Henry Clay was killed during the war and when Deely died shortly thereafter, proud Miss Emily was overcome with grief and remorse. She was a changed woman, but Harris's ironic theme is that the death of the two young people and the transformation of Emily Wornum had no visible effect on that other prideful woman, Feratia Bivins. Deely and Henry Clay had left a daughter, Pud Hon; and, when a much-subdued Mrs. Wornum came calling at Mrs. Bivins's and asked to see her granddaughter, Feratia cut her cold. " 'Hit's a sin to say it,' " Mrs. Bivins admits, but Miss Emily's presence rekindled all her old animosity and her resentment relative to the snubbing the Bivins family had received.

Feratia reconstructs the scene. First she hides Pud Hon in the shed; then picks up a " 'battlin'-stick' " that she always keeps close by; and, when Emily asks for admission, informs her with dripping sarcasm that she is " 'mighty proud to git calls from the big-bugs.' " Furthermore, she adds with beautiful effect, " 'If I had as much perliteness, ma'am, as I is cheers, I'd ast you to set down.' " When Feratia adamantly refuses to let Emily see her grandchild, she remarks that " 'things is come to a mighty purty pass when quality folks has to go frum house to house a-huntin' up pore white trash, an' a-astin' airter the'r kin.' " Emily manages to remain calm until she sees a childhood picture of Deely, whereupon she sinks to her knees with suddenly renewed grief. But Mrs. Bivins still cannot feel pity for Mrs. Wornum. Instead, she rises over the stricken woman and tells her that she can never be humble enough to go where Deely had gone; if it had not been for Deely, she adds grimly, " 'I'd 'a' strangled the life out'n you time your shadder darkened my door.' " What is more, Mrs. Bivins concludes angrily, if Emily so much as lays her little finger on Pud Hon, " *'I'll grab you by the goozle an' t'ar your haslet out.'* "

It is not the narrator but wise old Mingo who puts Mrs. Bivins's story into final perspective. The last section of Harris's tale is told almost entirely by the black man, who lingers with the narrator after Feratia leaves. Mingo explains that Mrs. Bivins had indeed " 'had bunnance er trouble' " in her time but that her behavior was to a considerable extent a function of her constitutional aversion to " 'big-bugs' " — to folks " 'w'at got Ferginny ways.' " The Bushrods, who were Miss Emily's people, were from Virginia; and Feratia " 'wouldn't 'a' stayed in a ten-acre fiel' wid um.' " Mingo, who agrees that the Bushrods were a headstrong clan, observes perceptively that Deely might not have married Henry Clay if it had not been for her Bushrod blood; and Mingo also reveals that Judge Wornum " 'tuck a fresh grip on de jimmy-john' " when Deely died, which accounted for his erratic behavior afterwards.

The weakest part of Harris's story may be Mingo's unswerving loyalty to what remained of his former master's family even after " 'de smash come' " and brought freedom in its wake. Mingo had shouldered his belongings and gone as far as the river before hearing Deely's voice in a dream, calling him back to take care of her daughter. So he went to Feratia's house and had ever since been helping her raise a small crop and provide for Pud Hon. One of the most persistent motifs in Harris's fiction, one based upon his own background, is that of the abandoned child who in time finds substitute parents; and Mingo serves in place of Pud Hon's dead father, while Feratia becomes her surrogate mother. Harris closes with a sentimental touch, which does not detract noticeably from the social realism of his story. Mingo notes that Pud Hon, who now has Deely's piano, has mysteriously begun playing most of the tunes her mother used to play. Although the old man pretends to have no idea where she learned them, it is obvious that Miss Deely's spirit has been imbibed by her daughter.

As critics have pointed out, Harris's Feratia Bivins is a vigorous and forceful woman who, though she may be poor, could hardly be termed "poor white trash." In his second story, however, which is long enough to be a novelette, Harris makes his portrait of mountaineer Teague Poteet seem a little more disreputable. Despite the story's attenuated length and its overplotting, *At Teague Poteet's: A Sketch of the Hog Mountain Range* has justly been called one of Harris's most socially authentic tales and one of the first studies of that distinctive class of rural American entrepreneurs, the moonshiners. Harris may have found the idea for his tale in the published testimony from an Atlanta trial in which two United States deputy marshalls were accused of having killed an old moonshiner, and the name Teague Poteet was apparently recommended to Harris as a good one to spin a moonshine story around.[12] Nonetheless, the final tale was Harris's alone.

As in "Mingo," Harris opens his story with a short essay about mutability, cultural change, and social dislocation in the South; and Harris cleverly uses the linguistic derivation of Teague Poteet's name to give the essay both structure and theme. "Emigration is a much more serious matter than revolution," Harris begins. "Virtually, it is obliteration." Thus the original Gérard Petit, a French settler who had landed on the coast of South Carolina in the colonial days, had pushed westward toward the mountains — and toward the gradual obliteration of his name and his cultural heritage. In the foothills of the Carolina mountains he encountered Englishmen moving to the South from Virginia and Pennsylvania, and the "*je, vous, nous* of France met in conflict with the 'ah-yi,' the 'we uns' and the 'you uns' " of the English. After marriages and time, "Jerd Poteet," as he was called by his neighbors, left a son patriotically named Huguenin Petit; and he in turn left Hugue Poteet as his heir. Hugue begot a child christened Hague, and Hague, "by some mysterious development of fate," left Teague Poteet in his place. While some of the Petits drifted into Alabama to become Pettys and Pettises, Teague Poteet found himself settling in 1859 on Hog Mountain outside of Gulletsville in North Georgia.[13] The forces of obliteration had done their work, and hardly a trace of his French lineage remained in the rough-shod and independent Teague Poteet.

Although Teague inadvertently earned Gulletsville's respect by knocking the county sheriff over the head with a chair, and by shooting a saloon-keeper who had been antagonizing the villagers, the mountain farmer decidedly did not like the flounces, starched collars, and equally starched "society" of the valley folk. Almost to spite the townspeople, and especially the uppity Gulletsville ladies, Teague married the lank and shiftless-looking Puss Pringle from Sugar Valley; and he had carried her into town for the ceremony behind him on his horse. Like Feratia Bivins, Teague and his wife — whose physical appearance belied her considerable energy and mental acuteness — had pride in their ways as mountain people. Chiefly, suggests Harris, the Poteets and the other dwellers on Hog Mountain believed themselves independent not only of the social but of the political concerns of the valley. When Fort Sumter fell and South Carolina withdrew from the Union, the townspeople were all astir with talk of Georgia's inevitable " 'se*say*sion.' " Teague only observed bluntly that " 'Them air Restercrats kin go wher' they dang please; I'm a-gwine to stay right slam-bang in the Nunited States.' " When Confederate conscript officers climbed the mountain to sign up the gaunt yet sturdy men who lived there, they were never heard from again. The valley soon learned to leave the strange breed of Union men alone in their upland hollows.

Teague's oblique feeling toward the Civil War was also owing to the birth of his first child, an event which coincided with the outbreak of hostilities. Watching his " 'gal-baby' " grow became Teague's all-consuming passion, but he realized after the war that his Sis, who was blossoming into a talented and radiantly beautiful woman, needed more education than the coarse, pipe-smoking mountain women could provide. " 'Sis hain't no dirt-eater,' " Teague observed, and he swallowed some of his pride and decided to send her into Gulletsville for schooling. Yet the money necessary to pay for Sis's education, to say nothing of her clothes, could not come from the meager yield of Teague's rocky farm. Harris, who maintains a slightly humorous and ironic narrative tone throughout his story, announces Teague's solution with a sardonic flourish: "... there is nothing more notorious in history, nothing more mysterious, than the fact that civilization is not over-nice in the choice of her handmaidens.... Every step in the advancement of the human race has a paradox of some kind as a basis. In the case of Sis Poteet, it was whiskey."

The results of Teague's erecting his still were several, and collectively they account for the remaining four-fifths of Harris's tale. First, Sis goes to school in Gulletsville and becomes the belle of the town. In the second place, "the breath of the Mountain" became so heavily charged with whiskey that "the Government got a whiff of it" and sent a posse of Revenue agents to investigate. Consistent with the violent and aggressive strain of independence that Teague and his fellow mountaineers possessed, however, the marshalls were ambushed, and three horses returned with empty saddles. When it came to moonshine, Teague and his men proved more loyal to their mountain kingdom than to the "Nunited States" herself.

The third consequence of Teague's illicit whiskey-making joins Sis and the government's designs on the mountain in an adventurous, and ultimately romantic, way; and Harris's pioneering work in the genre of the moonshiner-mountaineer tale unfortunately concludes with a sentimental plot-convention. In 1879 Washington sent tall, handsome, and self-possessed Philip Woodward to Gulletsville as an undercover agent who was to arrange for a secret raid on the mountain. Woodward, as it develops, had inherited some upland property in the vicinity, and he ostensibly called on Teague Poteet to verify its location. Although Harris again displays his masterful ear for dialect in Philip's conversations with various valley and mountain folk, and his eye for setting in his descriptions of scenes at the Poteets, the plot of his story now turns on Sis's and Philip's romantic involvement and on the crisis this relationship raised in Deputy Marshall Woodward's official assignment. Philip at length resigned his commission; and, when the government went ahead with its plans to raid the mountain, he steeled himself to fight alongside Teague and his allies. However, Harris avoids a morally complex issue by having the raid thwarted by a ruse.

The story regains some of its earlier realism when the federal raiders accidentally kill a mountain lad who is squirrel hunting and who is mistaken for an ambusher. Some weeks later, on the eve of Philip's and Sis Teague's wedding, the boy's distraught mother wounds the former deputy marshall, apparently believing him responsible for her son's death. Luckily Philip is only grazed, and he takes his new wife to live with him in Atlanta. There, Harris implies at the story's conclusion, an infusion of the mountain spirit will help to impart even more vigor to the developing New South. In a sense, then, the "obliteration" of the lineage of Gérard Petit is compensated for by the transformation of the South after the Civil War. Violence may attend the reconstitution of the South, and it seems to be basic to the poor-white mountaineer's code of behavior. But Harris, who fails to explore at any length the problem of violence in the South, emphasizes his favorite theme of reconciliation between South and North, and between the higher and the lower elements of society.

The remaining two stories in the *Mingo* collection are less ambitious pieces. "Blue Dave" is a portrait of a runaway slave that has disconcerted black critics because of its stereotypical Old South perspectives. Set again in Rockville, Putnam County, the story opens with an esthetic motif that suggests the mutability theme of Hawthorne's *House of the Seven Gables.* Hanging over the old and decaying Kendrick place is an "atmosphere of mystery" and a portentous silence; and the large fig tree that looms over the empty house is the only living reminder of a once-flourishing era when sermons were preached under its branches, marriages solemnized there, and duels fought in its shadow. Felix Kendrick had built the multigabled place in 1836 to show the community that " 'some folks was as good as other folks,' " as his father, old Grandsir Kendrick, had proudly phrased it.

As it turned out, young and ambitious Felix lived barely a dozen years in his showy mansion before his death. The story proper begins on the day of Felix's funeral in November 1849. Harris treats the reader to some delightful dialogue between old Brother

Johnny Roach and his neighbor Brother Brannum, the upshot of which is that the two village uncles hope that the funeral sermon will not be another one of those glib performances that claim " 'what thundering great men folks git to be arter they are dead.' " The two old friends pray that the preacher will be " 'jedgmatical enough for to let us off wi' the simple truth.' " Although the two cronies again serve effectively as the concluding chorus for the tale, the main part of Harris's story is a conventionalized throwback to the plantation ideal of the loyal but contented slave. Blue Dave, a powerfully built slave of supposedly magical powers who has succeeded in eluding his master, General Bledsoe, for five years, is seen watching the funeral from the gables of the house. Later he saves George Denham, the fiancé of Felix's daughter Kitty Kendrick, from flooded Murder Creek; and in appreciation Denham's family buys Blue Dave from Bledsoe for a thousand dollars. Blue Dave, who had always admired George, happily serves the family the rest of his days.

A variation on the theme of ownership and the building of family estates figures in "A Piece of Land." The setting is again Putnam County, more particularly the Pinetucky District, which prides itself on its honesty as well as on its sociability. However, Pinetucky is not proud of its richest resident, Bradley Gaither, whose greed for land and whose general surliness are an embarrassment to the district; in fact, Gaither's only redeeming trait is his beautiful daughter Rose. Gaither has succeeded in buying almost all the land he wanted except for the two-hundred-acre Carew place. But Old Billy Carew and his son Jack, whom Rose intends to marry, refuse to sell despite their great financial need. Then one day some of Gaither's cotton bales appear in the Carew barn; and, to Rose's dismay, Jack is convicted of theft and is sent to the state penitentiary at Milledgeville. A year later, on his deathbed, Gaither confesses that he had framed Jack. The story closes with another echo from Hawthorne's *House of the Seven Gables:* Rose and Jack will marry, and reconciliation between the Gaither and Carew families will at last be effected.

III Free Joe and Other Georgian Sketches *(1887)*

The title piece in Harris's second collection of magazine fiction has received more critical attention and has been more frequently anthologized than any of his local-color stories. "Free Joe and the

Rest of the World" is based upon fact, for young Harris had known not only freedman Free Joe when he lived in Eatonton but also "Free Joe's Cave," a local landmark. When Harris said that "Free Joe" was his favorite tale, he perhaps realized that he had achieved almost perfect esthetic balance among sentiment, tragedy, and realism in his study of the plight of a free black man who is alienated from the slave community as well as from the white man's world.

In 1840, Joe was the body-servant of Major Frampton, a cavalier, card-playing, slave-speculator who had chosen Hillsborough in Middle Georgia as his base of business operations. But Frampton lost almost everything one day during his famous poker game with Judge Alfred Wellington, a white-haired patriarch with mild blue eyes and gambling nerves that had been conditioned "during a long and arduous course of training from Saratoga to New Orleans." When Frampton had lost all but one Negro, Joe, he adjourned the game, signed Joe's free-papers, and, sauntering into a convenient pine thicket, blew out his brains. For several years Free Joe fared so well that he grew shiftless; for, since Judge Wellington now owned his wife, Lucinda, Joe chose the Judge as his guardian and was thus able to provide for himself. But, when the Judge died, Lucinda became the property of his half-brother, Calderwood, who was such a harsh master that his neighbors had nicknamed him "Spite."

Suddenly, Free Joe's easy life was over; for Spite Calderwood, who did not want any free Negroes on his farm, tore up Joe's free-pass when he came looking for his wife. Free Joe's presence in Hillsborough now began to trouble the townspeople also, for they regarded him as "the embodiment of that vague and mysterious danger that seemed to be forever lurking on the outskirts of slavery, ready to sound a shrill and ghostly signal in the impenetrable swamps, and steal forth under the midnight stars to murder, rapine, and pillage...."[14] Although Joe was by nature friendly, unassuming, and humble, he discovered that his freedom was now a kind of curse when he found himself around blacks or whites. "Having no owner," observes Harris, "every man was his master"; and, since the slaves on the Hillsborough farms and plantations now openly despised him, Joe sought at least a minimal kind of toleration from those whites who would talk to him. Ironically, Free Joe found the greatest sympathy among the poor whites, a class of people he had scorned when he was a slave. Becky and

Micajah Staley occasionally gave Joe a cup of coffee in return for a load of light-wood; they were glad to have him sit on the back steps of their cabin or at the foot of a big poplar tree that faced the Calderwood farm; and there Joe would drowse with his little dog, Dan, and listen for the sound of Lucinda's voice.

Joe soon discovered that he could send Dan to Calderwood's to bring Lucinda to see him; but, when Spite heard of their arrangement, he promptly took Lucinda to Macon and sold her. In some of the best writing in his entire canon, Harris recounts Joe's puzzlement and increasing loneliness when Lucinda repeatedly fails to come to him. Joe finally asks Becky Staley, who had a reputation as a fortune-teller, to read her cards and her coffee grounds in order to discover Lucinda's whereabouts. Joe grins with pleasure when Becky sees old Spite as the king of clubs and is delighted to learn that his Lucinda is the queen of spades: " 'Ef dat don't beat my time! De queen er spades! W'en Lucindy year dat hit'll tickle 'er, sho'!' " After Micajah corroborates what Becky had seen in her cards, namely that Lucinda has been taken away, Joe bids them goodnight and symbolically walks off into the darkness. For months he pays his nightly visit to the poplar tree, but he waits in vain. In time, Spite's dogs kill little Dan, but Joe keeps rationalizing that Dan will trot in some night soon, bringing Lucinda at his heels. Then one night in the fall Joe dozes off and does not awaken again. Harris cannot resist a sentimental closing tag: "A passer-by, glancing at him, could have no idea that such a humble creature had been summoned as a witness before the Lord God of Hosts."

Some black critics have found "Free Joe" disturbing because the story seems to argue that the Negro is better off as a slave than as a freeman, for he is ineffectual and pathetic when freedom is given to him. Yet this point of view overlooks the several factors that contribute to Joe's misfortune. Since Joe was not an ambitious or strong-willed individual to begin with, his shiftlessness was almost inevitable; and Lucinda's cruel sale down the river took what little resolve Joe had left after he found that most of the doors in the community were closed to him. With no skills to offer to the townspeople, and with nothing in which to take pride, Free Joe became a useless appendage and an outcast from the world of men. A type of outcast himself, Harris identified with his protagonist and realized that Free Joe's death was the esthetically and emotionally inevitable conclusion to this tale of social realism.

A somewhat more romantic story that functions in suggestive

counterpoint to "Free Joe" is "Rosalie," a controversial tale about a beautiful octoroon that Harris never collected after its publication in *Century* in 1901.[15] Rosalie is the passionate, vivacious, and articulate housemaid of the Widow Awtry of Shady Dale, Jasper County.[16] Proud of her near-white status, she flaunts it by always dressing in white; but she errs fatally when she impetuously falls in love with her mistress's son, Arthur Hutchinson. As was Madam Awtry originally, Hutchinson is a Northerner; however, his total commitment to the Abolitionist cause seems irrational to his aunt and to her Shady Dale friends.

Echoing one of the themes in "Free Joe," a theme that Harris himself espoused in his more conservative moments, Madam Awtry asks Arthur what good emancipation would do if it meant that unskilled and uneducated Negroes would be left to fend for themselves. But the undaunted Hutchinson, oblivious of Rosalie's passion for him, uses her to spread the word among the slaves in the community that a meeting to plan an insurrection would be held the following Saturday. Although Rosalie blindly complies with everything Arthur requests of her, she soon has misgivings about his plan and tells the whites what is in store. Rosalie feels only contempt for the black slaves; however, her decision to reveal the plot is primarily the result of her anger that Hutchinson apparently has no personal interest in her. When Rosalie learns that the whites will attack Hutchinson with force on Saturday night, her passionate love for him resumes its sway. She runs to warn him and saves his life, but in the process is accidentally shot in the heart.

Harris's rather obvious symbolism in the story reinforces its racial themes. Rosalie's name is a kind of pun, for she always insists upon wearing a red rose on the breast of her white dress. The night of her death she had angrily flung away her rose when she thought about her thwarted love for Arthur; and, when she is killed, her blood stains her dress where the flower would have been. Perhaps Harris was reluctant to collect his tale because of its double-miscegenation theme, despite the fact that the octoroon's attempt to be even more "white" and to indulge in passion for a white man is firmly denied by the fact of her death. Harris, who disliked violence and who always regretted that it took a Civil War to resolve the problem of slavery, would, like Rosalie, have been philosophically opposed to slave rebellions. Yet Rosalie's violent death functions much like Free Joe's more peaceful one as a reminder that the black person caught between two worlds, as the impetuous Rosalie and the outcast freedman surely are, finally has no place to turn.

"Little Compton" and "Aunt Fountain's Prisoner," two of Harris's Civil War stories that proved most popular with his contemporaries, treat his continuing editorial theme of North-South reconciliation. Harris never fought in the war nor researched its history with any thoroughness; and, although he occasionally tries to reconstruct a battle scene in his fiction, he generally prefers to focus on the social or economic climate that accompanies it. Such is the case in these tales. Little Compton, a genial and fair-minded New Jersey man, opened a small grocery business in Hillsborough, Putnam County, in 1850; and he endeared himself to the community by tolerating a variety of practical jokes and other pranks designed to make fun of a transplanted Yankee. When the war broke out, however, he felt a moral obligation to fight on the Union side.

Harris paints a sensitive portrait of the rising tensions in the pro-slavery community on the eve of the war, particularly in his account of the lampblacking of an Abolitionist who is tied up and sent to the next town sporting a sign "Abolitionist! Pass Him On, Boys." The plot of the story turns on the fact that Little Compton and his best friend from Hillsborough, Jack Walthall, coincidentally lose their arms when the same bullet hits them at Gettysburg. Compton is taken prisoner; and, while he is recuperating in Hillsborough, he once saves Jack from an irate German mercenary who is serving in Sherman's army. The friendship of Jack and Little Compton, Harris concludes with fanfare, is "prophetic of the days to come, when peace and fraternity should seize upon the land, and bring unity, happiness, and prosperity to the people."

"Aunt Fountain's Prisoner" opens as "Mingo" had with a rehearsal of the first-person narrator's boyhood memories of Rockville and his thoughts about the changes the war had wrought on the townspeople. He is delighted to see that vigorous old Aunt Fountain still peddles her ginger-cakes and persimmon beer on the town square, and he hears from this independent old black woman the story of her role in the conversion of the Tomlinson plantation into a profitable business after the war. When Sherman's army passed through the town, Aunt Fountain explains, she had been in her usual place on the square. A Union soldier who had come by had told her that she was now free — at which point he had helped himself to the rest of her ginger-cakes. Aunt Fountain, who was furious, had told him, " 'Ef I wuz free ez you is, suh, I'd fling you down en take dem ginger-cakes 'way fum you.' " Aunt Fountain had then walked around for awhile to cool her anger until she accidentally discovered a wounded Yankee in a ditch. She brought Ferris Trunion to the Tomlinson place as her "prisoner," where she helped to nurse him back to health. After the war, Ferris married the Tomlinson's daughter; and, being a practical-minded and a progressive adopted son of the New South, he soon transformed the war-ravaged plantation into a prosperous dairy farm.

The romantic involvement of a Yankee and a Southerner is a recurring motif in Harris's short fiction. He first used it in his revised narrative about Uncle Remus's battle experiences, "A Story of the War" (1880), and normally it symbolizes the peaceful reconciliation of North and South. Despite Harris's public posture as a meliorist, he was naturally aware of the lingering Southern resentment toward the North after the war and of the social conflicts that this resentment could produce. Harris uses a North-South romance ironically in "Trouble on Lost Mountain" and in the novelette *Azalia* to explore some of the social complexities and conflicts that he saw.

"Trouble on Lost Mountain" is reminiscent of *At Teague Poteet's* in its delightful portraits of Georgia mountaineers, but it concludes on a tragic note. Beautiful and impulsive Babe Hightower of Lost Mountain, whose father Abe illegally brews beer and consequently has to be on the lookout for Revenuers, falls in love with a handsome Northerner who has come to locate potential marble quarries in the area. Chichester, an engineer, geologist, and, in short, another of the new breed of postwar "general-utility" men like Ferris Trunion, keeps his plans secret because he knows of the mountain people's pride in their region and of their suspiciousness about Northern schemes for building railroads and "a-fetchin' destruction" to their homeland. Although Chichester is initially warned to stay off the "mounting" unless he wants to catch a case of Hightower "measles" (buckshot wounds), he gradually wins over the mountaineers — except for the jealous Tuck Peevy, Babe's former beau. One night when Babe and Chichester are sitting on the Hightower porch, Tuck shoots at Chichester's hat but accidentally kills Babe, who had been playfully wearing the hat at the time. Chichester, shocked and dismayed, leaves the mountain forever; behind him, gaunt Tuck Peevy spends his days trying to manage the Hightower farm and tend to old Abe, whose mind snapped when his daughter died. The unrelieved grimness that closes his tale is unusual for Harris, and it reveals a dimension of his literary vision that many critics have overlooked.

Azalia opens with a Jamesian flair. The fall of 1873 found Boston suffering from the cold, and young and attractive Helen Eustis, whose health had deteriorated after she lost her brother in the Civil War and then her father in 1867, has been ordered by her doctor to go to Middle Georgia for a rest cure. When her father's health had begun to fail eight years earlier, Helen had accompanied him on a two-year trip through Europe; but, Harris editorializes, she had returned to the United States convinced that, although some things in Europe and England were worth being impressed by, America herself was not a "barren waste" just because her institutions did not yet bear the seal of antiquity. Helen had the "genuine American spirit," Harris declares: hers was a mixture of provinciality, patriotism, and originality. In other words, she would serve as the perfect Northern envoy to the South.

As Harris does in most of his short stories, he enjoys portraying the comic interludes in human affairs. Helen and her maiden aunt, Harriet Tewksbury, who was occupying herself by turns with Spiritualism and with women's rights, agree that Georgia would be preferable to Florida. Although a little concerned about the machinations of the Ku Klux Klan in Georgia, they definitely avoid visiting Florida; for the people they knew who had come from there were fatigued, and, notes Helen, " 'something in their attitude and appearance seemed to suggest that they had seen the sea-serpent.' " As the two women travel by train towards Azalia, Georgia, they are entertained by a "Southron" book salesman peddling Civil War histories and other narratives; and, while Helen tries to remain more open-minded, crotchety Aunt Harriet criticizes the "arrested development," barbarism, and shiftlessness of the South.

By the end of the novelette, the reader learns that Helen's brother had been buried nearby, alongside a dead Confederate boy; and Helen predictably marries a handsome Southerner, General Peyton Garwood. The marriage occurs in Boston, and the social column of one of the papers headlines the event "Practical Reconstruction." Yet the most impressive and realistic portion of the narrative, which Harris based partly on an actual occurrence, features an ironic inversion of the "Practical Reconstruction" theme. Emma Jane Stucky and her simple-minded son, Bud, are poor-white "Tackies" who live on the outskirts of Azalia. Pathetic in their poverty and their ignorance, the Tackies nevertheless have their pride and normally keep their distance from the townspeople. When poor Bud also falls in love with the charming Northern visitor Helen, whose organ-playing haunts him, the results can only be unfortunate. Harris may be guilty of condescending sentimentality in allowing Bud to waste away and finally die of grief when he learns that Helen loves Garwood instead of him. But there is poignant psychological and social realism in the bitter rhetorical question that Emma Jane Stucky puts to Helen, who weeps when she sees Bud die and who realizes that there was no way she could have resolved his emotional crisis. " 'Whatter you cryin' fer now?' " Emma Jane asks her bluntly. " 'You wouldn't a-wiped your feet on 'im. Ef you wuz gwine ter cry, whyn't you let 'im see you do it 'fore he died? What good do it do 'im now? He wa'n't made out'n i'on like me.' " A short while later Emma Jane's pride and strong will have gone slack, however, and sorrow has "dimmed the fire of her eyes." The last we see of her, the poor woman feebly takes Helen to view the pathetic shrine she has erected to her son's memory: a flimsy wooden box around one of his footprints.

IV   Balaam and His Master and Other Stories and Sketches *(1891)*

Three of the stories in the *Balaam and His Master* collection are portraits of slaves, or of former slaves who, like Mingo, reveal a capacity for love and loyalty, or qualities of insight, that are greater than those of the white people around them. Of course, among some of Harris's critics and interpreters loyalty on the part of the black man or woman can also be construed as racial subservience. But the fact remains that Harris's Negroes, like Faulkner's, often evince the ability to endure, even if their endurance involves playing certain kinds of roles in the white man's world. The fearless black valet Balaam in the title story, for example, is the only person who can control his impetuous and bad-tempered master, Berrien Cozart. Balaam supports and assists his master through fights and gambling disasters; however, when Berrien is arrested after shooting a sheriff and dies in his hometown jail, he is finally beyond his servant's help.

"Ananias" is a more ambiguous study of a black man's efforts to keep his former master, Colonel Flewellen, and his daughter Nelly solvent after the Civil War had brought economic desolation to Middle Georgia. Believing that Flewellen's one-time plantation overseer, who is now a merchant and to whom Flewellen is heavily in debt, is somehow cheating the colonel, Ananias gladly steals from him. Ananias is accused of theft, but Harris sidesteps some troublesome moral questions by having the black man freed on a technicality.

"Mom Bi: Her Friends and Enemies" is a warm portrait of a Gullah mammy from the "sandhill" farm country of South Carolina. Quarrelsome, officious, opinionated, and visibly proud of her social status in the Waynecroft household as compared to that of the poor-white sandhillers, Mom Bi was nevertheless a likable and generous person who suffered with the Waynecrofts when they lost their son Gabriel during the war. Afterwards, she went to Savannah to nurse her stricken daughter during the smallpox epidemic; when her daughter died, Mom Bi came back to her former master's house to look once more upon Gabriel's portrait, and then to die. Mom Bi, Harris implies, knew what it meant to be a servant of mankind.

Harris treats one of his favorite subjects, a family's relationship to the land, in "The Old Bascom Place." As in "A Piece of Land" in the *Mingo* volume, this lengthy tale has disinheritance as a theme; but, in this case, a combination of the collapse of the Southern economy after the war and Briscoe Bascom's extravagant wife causes the Bascoms to lose their old plantation to another of Harris's progressive Yankees, Francis Underwood. When old Bascom and his daughter Mildred grow poorer and poorer, Mildred, as well as the townspeople, becomes concerned when the old man begins to suffer delusions that he still owns the plantation and can sit on the veranda whenever he wishes. Harris resolves the crisis with his standard yoking of North and South: Underwood is happy to let Bascom sit on the porch and dream old dreams, and he will in time marry Mildred and make her father's delusions real.

The most accomplished and the most socially significant tales in *Balaam and His Master* are "A Conscript's Christmas" and "Where's Duncan?" The former story presents a view of the Civil War that is not normally found in Southern fiction, but Harris's plotting detracts somewhat from the tale's social realism. The setting is Sugar Mountain, Georgia, in December 1863; the Confederacy has seen its armies weakened by the long struggle; and orders have been issued to draft all available men. However, Captain Moseley and Private Chadwick, two conscript officers, find that the folks on Sugar Mountain are in no mood to have the young man they are seeking, Israel Spurlock, taken off to fight. Israel, a peace-loving youth and his poor mother's only help, is about to be married to Polly, a pretty mountain lass. Harris develops a whole gallery of Dickensian characters in his tale, from a shrill-voiced old man who protests the Confederacy's forcing people to fight, to a powerful hunchback, Danny Lemmons, who masterminds delaying strategies to keep the soldiers off-balance and confused about Israel's whereabouts. The story is resolved in favor of the mountain people: the two conscript officers are eventually pacified and enjoy the Christmas Day wedding feast; and a jealous rival for Polly's hand, who later tries to lead a detachment of soldiers up the mountain to seize Israel, is killed by Danny Lemmons when he fires at the mountaineers. Echoing themes in *At Teague Poteet's* and "Trouble on Lost Mountain," Harris again insists on the fierce independence of the Georgia mountain people.

Although Harris chose not to reprint "Rosalie," he did include "Where's Duncan?", another tale of miscegenation, in the *Balaam* collection. Probably because of its controversial theme, Harris opens his story with an apology by the first-person narrator for the "uncertain flight" that he will be sharing with the reader; and old Isaiah Winchell also admits that the tale he will tell has "pestered me at times when I ought to have been in my bed and sound asleep." Old man Winchell sees his tale as a kind of Gothic ghost story, but Harris's vivid imagery and the believable circumstances surrounding the narrative bring it very much into the real world. Harris's story, furthermore, is an intriguing prefiguration of several themes and images in Faulkner's *Light in August* and *Absalom, Absalom!*

In 1826, when on his way to Augusta with a load of cotton, Isaiah had met a dark-featured vagabond named Willis Featherstone. That evening, when Willis played the fiddle for the Negroes gathered around the cluster of cotton-wagons, Isaiah said he made one dream strange dreams. Willis explained that his journey was going to end the following night near the Sandhills, and he gave the narrator both a riddle and its answer. A father had a son, sent him to school, but grew to hate him and finally sold him to a Negro speculator. Where was the son's mother? In the riddle, in the riddle, closed Featherstone enigmatically. The next night the cotton caravan stopped near a plantation house, and a tall mulatto woman with straight black hair who came to listen intently to Willis's fiddle-playing said that Giles Featherstone had invited them all to come up to his house, but she warned them not to go. At this point Willis abruptly asked the woman, "Where's Duncan?" and she broke down and said that he had been sold. Harris concludes his tale with a lurid Gothic scene: later that night the plantation house caught fire, and through the dining-room window the narrator saw the mulatto woman stab an old white man with a carving knife. After she shrieked once, "Where's Duncan?" the burning roof collapsed on the struggling figures. One observer insisted that he saw Willis in the dining room enjoying the spectacle, but Harris leaves this element ambiguous. All Isaiah knew was that Willis was never seen again — and that to this day he still smelled the burning human flesh.

Harris's closing symbolism suggests that the fires of damnation both literally and figuratively consumed the Featherstones. Appropriately, old Giles experienced a kind of double death — at the hands of the woman he had used and also in the flames. By keeping Willis's fate ambiguous, furthermore, Harris raises the rhetorical question: what price must black children pay for the sins of white fathers? Yet the story may also be a psychologically complex projection of some of Harris's own deep-seated anxieties and insecurities. After all, Harris himself was a bastard child, abandoned by his father. Like Willis Featherstone, Harris must have often reflected upon the fact that he had no family traditions to draw upon from the past and no legitimate identity in the present.

V Tales of the Home Folks in Peace and War *(1898)*

Two of the twelve stories in the collection *Tales of the Home Folks in Peace and War,* "The Late Mr. Watkins of Georgia" and "A Belle of St. Valerien," were discussed in the second chapter. Of the remaining stories, several are sentimental or romantically adventurous pieces that need only brief attention. "How Whalebone Caused a Wedding," for example, is essentially an extended anecdote about how the skill of Whalebone, the foxhound, won a wager and helped bring a young lady and her chosen man together. "A Run of Luck," which is reminiscent of "Balaam and His Master," recounts the postwar horse-racing and gambling escapades of a young white man, Linton Moreland, and the old Negro servant, Primus, who remains loyal to him. The story ends with Linton's braving a steamboat fire to rescue the daughter of a man who had just accused him of cheating; and, predictably, Linton later marries the girl. Observing how panic-stricken the girl's normally aloof and self-contained father had become during the fire, old Primus concludes: " '. . . ef you take proudness out'n de white folks dey er des ez skeery ez de niggers.' "

The black man's loyalty to the white is also the theme of "The Colonel's Nigger Dog," but in this tale, which is set in pre-Emancipation days, the white master at least feels guilty about the way he treats his slave. Before she died, Mrs. Rivers of Jasper County had stipulated that Shadrack, or Uncle Shade as he was commonly known, always be treated well by the family. Her son the colonel later became irritated by Uncle Shade's pride in his favored position as a slave, and he trained a dog to hunt him down when Shade ran off after an argument. After old Shade was caught, he reminded the colonel of the fishing and the quartz-hunting they had done together in the old days; the colonel relented and only told the neighbors that he had been out training his "nigger dog."

In three stories in the volume, an infant child is at the center of plot and sentiment. In "A Baby in the Siege" and "The Baby's Fortune" Harris spins an elaborate and somewhat preposterous plot around three characters he had introduced in "A Conscript's Christmas," one of the *Balaam* tales. Captain Moseley and Private Chadwick, now part of the defensive perimeter in the siege of Atlanta, learn that the hunchback Danny Lemmons is married and working as a Union spy in the city and that he wants to take his newborn child away from his wife, Cassy, because of a quarrel they had had. But an exploding shell fortuitously kills Danny, and unbelievably, another crashing shell later reveals a considerable amount of money hidden years earlier in the house where Cassy and her baby are residing. After the war, Private Chadwick and Cassy, now well-set, marry and live in Atlanta. In "The Baby's Christmas" Harris uses a child as a motif for reconciliation between a proud mother and a daughter whom the mother had disowned because she had married below her station; and a loyal and sensitive black cook helps to effect the reconciliation.

Harris returns to his earlier theme of the conscription of Confederate soldiers in "A Bold Deserter," although this time the peace-loving lad sought by the conscript officer is sent to the battle front. When he learns that his mother is sick, young Billy Cochran deserts and returns home; but he later proves himself in battle and eventually becomes commander of a regiment.[17] In an interlocked collection of five Civil War sketches that is entitled "The Comedy of War," "On the Union Side," "On the Confederate Side," "On Neutral Ground," "Commerce and Sentiment," and "The Curtain Falls," Harris uses a less conventional formula but one of his standard themes. On a skirmish line between the two warring armies, Private O'Halloran, a Yankee sharpshooter whose Irish brogue Harris writes as effortlessly and as accurately as he does Middle Georgia dialect, and his commanding officer, Captain Fambrough, arrange a short truce with their three Confederate adversaries in order to conduct some "grocery business." After Confederate tobacco is swapped for Union tea and sugar, the five soldiers become friendly with one another. Nearby, Captain Fambrough's stubborn father and his sister Julia are still occupying the family home; Julia had met one of the Confederate officers earlier; and, just as a courier arrives to announce Lee's surrender, Julia and the Southern officer, Lieutenant Clopton, declare their love. Thus two men who might have killed each other will now become brothers-in-law.

War and marriage are also the themes of a related story with a punning title, "An Ambuscade." Jack Kilpatrick, who was a Confederate sharpshooter in "The Comedy of War," is wounded in the Battle of Atlanta and taken to his family home for attention. Jack's new Yankee friend, O'Halloran, obtains a talented Union surgeon for him by pretending that he is a wounded Northern officer. Parallel to the earlier tale, the Yankee surgeon falls in love with Jack's sister Flora and marries her after the war.

The best of the stories in *Tales of the Home Folks*, and one of the most intriguing of all of Harris's local-color tales, is "The Cause of the Difficulty." Although set during the Civil War, Harris ironically notes that the "noxious vapors" of that struggle were thinner in the mountains of Northeast Georgia where his story takes place; for, though the war itself may have been distant, Harris's tale is nevertheless one about the violent passions that lurk in human beings. The first-person narrator relates the true account of Toog Parmalee's murder of his sweetheart, commenting that the newspaper reports of the event proved inaccurate when compared with the version he learned from old Mrs. Pruett of Tray Mountain. As Harris so often does in his writings, he anchors his tale squarely in the middle of the oral tradition of the people. And in a subtle jibe at his own profession as a journalist, Harris lets Mrs. Pruett correct errors of both fact and motive in the "official" newspaper accounts of the murder.

Mrs. Pruett explains that the murder took place not in the "Hatcher's Ford" neighborhood, as the newspapers stated, but at Hatch's Clearing; a more important corrective, however, is that Toog Parmalee was not temporarily insane when he killed his girl friend. " 'What's bred in the bone will come out in the blood,' " the old lady observes pithily; furthermore, she suggests, the story of Toog Parmalee is really the story of his mother, Loorany. Loorany Parmalee was once the chief attraction in the area; while rough around the edges, she was a handsome woman and a passionate, willful one. Mrs. Pruett saw Loorany flirting with a Mr. Hildreth of a neighboring county, even though it was well known that John Wesley Millirons was in love with her. Although Mrs. Pruett warned Millirons that he was losing Loorany, he did not seem especially worried. Soon everyone thought that Hildreth intended to marry Loorany, and she was naturally upset when she learned that he was not going to do so. Mrs. Pruett recreates the climactic scene. Learning of Hildreth's decision, John Wesley takes his rifle and starts to shoot him when suddenly Loorany, breathing hard, does it instead. Afterwards, she asks John Wesley if he will take her "just as she is"; he says yes and soon marries her.

Harris's sense of delicacy forbade his elaborating the details of what the concluding episode confirms has been a story of seduction and abandonment: soon after Hildreth's death, Loorany Parmalee Millirons dies in giving birth to a boy who would be named Toog Parmalee. Once again, the theme of illegitimate birth and the wages of sin seems to be a conscious or unconscious reflection of Harris's continuing introspection about Mary Harris's passion and its subsequent effects on his life and personality. Mrs. Pruett concludes that Toog Parmalee shot his sweetheart because his mother had shot hers; Loorany's passionate nature had been bred into her son, Mrs. Pruett suggests, and he could not escape his heritage.

All of these things, then, were collectively the "cause of the difficulty" reported in the papers. " 'Thribble the generations,' " she adds, " 'an' sin's arm is long enough to retch through 'em all.' " What is suggestive about Mrs. Pruett's tale is that it not only projects aspects of Harris's own psyche but also implies the universality of evil. For, if Loorany and her son were guilty of an excess of passion that came out "in the blood," so, too, was Hildreth — and probably Toog's sweetheart, as well.

VI   The Making of a Statesman and Other Stories *(1902)*

Harris's humor and dialect portraits redeem three otherwise weak stories in *The Making of a Statesman.* "Miss Puss's Parasol" is a comic and sentimental tale about how Aunt Minervy Ann used a series of tricks, as well as cajolery, to bring shy Judge Ballard and equally reticent Miss Puss Gresham together. "A Child of Christmas: A Christmas Tale of North and South" is reminiscent of "A Belle of St. Valerien" in its use of French-Canadian and of Georgian characters and dialect. The opening section of the story is effectively told by a French-Canadian narrator, whose dialect seems as natural as Billy Sanders's in later parts of the tale. If Harris's Essie was his source for the Canadian dialect, there is no doubt something of their own love story in the tale; for Harris describes how young and attractive Zepherine Dion comes to Shady Dale from Quebec to serve as a female companion to Sarah Clopton. By the end of the tale, Zepherine has been proposed to by local Dr. Dorrington; moreover, in a variation of a favorite Harris theme, she has also been reunited with her father, who had left his family years earlier and was found living in New Orleans.

"Flingin' Jim and His Fool-Killer" has a somewhat contrived plot but is a good study in black dialect and an interesting variant in the lore of the fool-killer, a folk tradition that apparently originated in North Carolina.[18] In the early 1870s, at the depot in Harmony Grove, Middle Georgia, a self-possessed Negro boy is exchanging some banter with an older black man who tries to intimidate the lad by saying that he is a "blue-gum nigger." Negroes with blue gums were said to have a poisonous bite, but the young boy, whose name is Flingin' Jim because of his skill with his throwing arm, is not scared by the older man. When a tall, dark-haired stranger arrives on the train and asks to be taken to the old Moseley place, Flingin' Jim gives him a ride in his buggy and explains that for years his family has been waiting for Marse Phil Moseley to return to the old plantation, which is now about to be sold for taxes.

The stranger acknowledges that he used to know Phil Moseley, but that he was now dead — although not buried. Ann Briscoe, who had been in love with Phil, was managing the old plantation and had spent many lonely years wondering why Phil had not answered her love letters. Of course, the handsome stranger proves to be Phil himself, who had become emotionally "dead" over the years because he had wondered why Ann had failed to answer his letters. It turns out that both sets of letters had been intercepted by Bill Dukes, a rival of Phil's, and by his brother Tom. In a show-down between Moseley and the Dukes boys, Flingin' Jim, who had once saved Ann from a tramp with a well-thrown grapeshot, comes to Phil's assistance and knocks Bill Dukes out with another throw of his "fool-killer" (the North Carolina folk hero used a club to brain fools and obfuscators). Naturally, the two lovers are recon-ciled at the end of the tale.

The title story in the volume is in some ways a surprisingly modern one, for it anticipates the political ghost-writing and king-making practices of our own time. Harris maintains a slightly ironic tone throughout "The Making of a Statesman" that effec-tively reinforces the story's sardonic theme. Mary Lou Feather-stone, who believes that her husband Meredith has political poten-tial, does her best to build ambition into him. She takes him to commencement exercises at the University of Virginia and at Har-vard, and she selects books to inspire and challenge him. But it takes bright young Billy Spence, an orphan living in Hillsborough who liked the Featherstones and their eleven-year-old daughter Emily, to make Featherstone's political fortune. Billy Spence was essentially a misplaced romantic who loved the ideals of chivalry, especially the notion of bestowing honor on a lady like Mary Lou or on her daughter, more than he did any thought of his own per-sonal success or profit. So he set about tutoring Meredith Feather-stone, but he also coached him in oratory and even wrote speeches for him when necessary.

Featherstone soon rose to an important position in the state senate and later in the Confederate House of Congress, and his wife died proud of her husband's success but ignorant of Billy's role in it. Yet, when Meredith passed away in the 1870s, he was a strangely embittered man; and his daughter Emily, now a young woman of twenty-four, soon found out why. In looking through her father's papers, she learned that Billy had secretly sacrificed his own identity and ambition for her father, her mother, and herself. When Emily seeks Billy, she finds him suffering from a fever and exhausted from the years of strain and bottled-up tension. Harris's standard concluding motif — that Emily will nurse Billy back to health and probably marry him — detracts only slightly from an otherwise politically and psychologically sensitive tale about two men who lived lives of false identity. In "The Making of a Statesman," as in "Mingo," "Free Joe," and several other stories, Harris's insight into the emotional and psychological makeup of men and women carries his fiction beyond its occasional conventionalisms into the realm of real literary art.

CHAPTER 6

Chronicles and Novels

I Harris and Extended Narrative

HARRIS'S journalistic background as a paragrapher, editorial writer, and sketcher of character and scene predisposed him to write short stories when he tried his hand at fiction. The oral tradition in which Harris was steeped reinforced his tendency to compose in shorter units; but, at the same time, Harris was responsive to cyclical and episodical patterns in narrative and was not reluctant upon occasion to try linking episodes together to produce longer works. The autobiographical *On the Plantation* (1892) is a relatively coherent piece of extended narrative; and, as we have seen, stories like *At Teague Poteet's* and *Azalia* are long enough to be termed novelettes. Furthermore, one of Harris's earliest attempts at writing fiction, the serialized *Romance of Rockville* (1878), is a legitimate venture into the novel genre.

Despite his interest in longer forms of narrative, Harris apologized for the "gaps and lapses" in *Sister Jane* (1896) and for the "loose ends" of *Gabriel Tolliver* (1902), and he acknowledged that novel-writing was not his strong suit. The few critics who have discussed Harris's novels in any detail generally agree with his self-assessment, but they readily give him credit for the things he does well in his longer works: developing realistically the socioeconomic milieu and, as he always seems to do, creating living characters. Reviewers in the early 1900s, as well as more recent critics, have found *Gabriel Tolliver* a valuable portrait of the Reconstruction era[1]; additionally, Harris's use of ironic first-person narration is a strikingly modern technique in *Sister Jane*. Many readers believe that Billy Sanders, the cornfield philosopher and narrator, ranks equally with Uncle Remus as a fully realized character. And another of Harris's late creations, Aunt Minervy Ann, is a delightfully vivid personality whose *Chronicles* are among the most humorous and engaging of Harris's works.

II   The Romance of Rockville *(1878)*

In writing his first extended narrative, Harris made the mistakes that the fledgling novelist might be expected to make. Primarily, he kept too many skeletons hidden in the closet until the end of the novel, thus making plot development cumbersome in the earlier chapters; and he settled for romantic and sentimental conventions instead of trying for originality. Yet, ironically, the convention that Harris relied on most heavily was one that echoed a crisis in his own life. Fatherless himself, Harris made the restitution of an orphaned boy to his family his major theme; and the death of an illegitimate child is also an important motif in the plot. Another intriguing psychological image of the author is William Wornum, the schoolmaster. Harris developed Wornum more completely as a persona in *Sister Jane,* the next novel; for he plays only a minor role in *The Romance of Rockville.* Like Harris, Wornum is diffident, self-conscious around women, and something of a loner.

The Romance of Rockville actually begins seven or eight years prior to the opening scene. In 1840 or 1841 the worthless white trash Jim Ashfield had kidnapped the infant child of Judge Walthall and had burned down his house. A year later a child that Ashfield said was the Walthalls' was returned to them, but it soon died. During the well-written and dramatic trial scene that closes the novel, the reader learns that the baby that had died was actually the illegitimate son of Cindy Ashfield, Jim's sister. The Walthall child had been rescued from the cruel kidnapper and reared by none other than Calhoun Walthall, the judge's long-lost brother. When Calhoun discovered his nephew's identity, he returned him to his proper father; and Ashfield was sentenced for his crime.

Harris compensates for the improbabilities in his tale with his relaxed but often psychologically incisive narrative commentary about the inhabitants of Rockville. He gives the flavor of provincial life in a Southern town, and even in this early work his characters are speaking the vernacular convincingly. Some of Harris's actors hover between the stereotypical and the real: Nora Perryman, for instance, the beautiful and intelligent blind girl secretly loved by several men in town, including Wornum; or Tiny Padgett, the alcoholic village poet who has one day of glory as lawyer for the prosecution of Ashfield and then commits suicide when he realizes that Nora prefers Wornum to him. But William Wornum and Miss Jane Perryman, Nora's older sister famous for her trenchant tongue as well as for her generosity, are authentic figures whom Harris keeps in focus throughout his novel.

Miss Jane, an aggressive conversationalist and gossip, prides herself on her knowledge of human nature and enjoys vanquishing opponents with her homely aphorisms. For instance, when the schoolmaster unjustly criticizes someone he does not know, she observes wryly that " 'You don't have to ketch a frog on the jump to cripple it.' " Of another character's misguided sense of charity she protests that " 'A hen that lays in another hen's nest don't hatch many chickens.' "[2] Miss Jane does not play a central role in the plot of the novel, but Harris brings her to life in depicting her likable obstreperousness. Wornum's sardonic sense of humor and his melancholic preoccupation with his own lack of visibility or ambition in life help to round out his portrait and also reflect Harris's concerns about his own role and identity. Harris ends his book by bringing Wornum back into humanity's fold, for he hints that he has at last learned how to express his love for Nora and will in time ask her for her hand.

III   Sister Jane: Her Friends and Acquaintances. A Narrative
of Certain Events and Episodes Transcribed from the Papers
of the Late William Wornum *(1896)*

As the above rambling title suggests, Harris's second novel is a leisurely narrative filtered through the consciousness of a persona; Wornum the narrator is clearly a Harris self-portrait. At the time, Harris confessed to a friend with only a little exaggeration that if readers found out who Wornum was it would have "ruined" him.[3] As Cousins has demonstrated, there are considerable parallels between the novel and Harris's own life.[4] The story begins in 1848, the year of Harris's birth; Hallyton, where the tale is set, could easily be the village of Eatonton; Wornum's sister Jane, who the narrator admits was the "only mother I had ever known," maintains a small tailoring shop as Harris's mother had; the basic plot of the story, the question of the paternity of Mandy Satterlee's illegitimate male child, parallels Mary Harris's problem when she moved to Eatonton. Finally, both Wornum and Harris were self-effacing, especially around women; lacked assertiveness and confidence; and enjoyed reading Sir Thomas Browne, Montaigne, Shakespeare, and the Bible.

Harris may very well have been trying consciously or unconsciously to purge himself of personal anxieties by writing *Sister Jane,* and the book is a psychologically complex piece of semiautobiography. Nevertheless, Harris is able to maintain enough esthetic and ironic distance from his narrator to give him a "life" separate from the author's own. William is something of a recluse: thirty-five or forty years old and a bachelor, he is "enamored of solitude," especially the seclusion of his "snug little room" behind his side porch — which itself is shielded from view by honeysuckle vines. From his retreat Wornum writes of a series of events that befell his household in the late 1840s and early 1850s; these were precipitated by Jane's deciding to take care of Mandy Satterlee and her baby, who are quite literally found on the Wornum front porch during a winter storm. Mandy is an uneducated white trash whose history consists of one misfortune after another; yet, as had Mary Harris, she honestly wants to make a new start and is eager to work for her room and board.

A subplot of William's narrative is his own hesitantly told story about his repressed love for Mary Bullard, the attractive daughter of Colonel Bullard, his aloof and aristocratic neighbor. Mary had been William's childhood sweetheart; but, after she had grown up and gone off to college and then returned home to live with her parents, he did not know how to reestablish a relationship with her. Feeling awkward, he tried to avoid her even though she was as natural and charming as she had been as a young girl. So Wornum, who substituted voyeurism for real human contact, began watching Mary through his honeysuckle hedge (there is a little Freudianism in this motif). He feels uneasy about his behavior, but does not know what to do about it. When he desires human society, Harris reveals with some psychological acuteness, Wornum prefers to chat with older inhabitants of the village like Mrs. Sally Beshears and her aged sisters, Miss Polly and Miss Becky Pike. He feels comfortable around these ladies and unthreatened by them until they start making oblique references to a "certain person" who should take Mary Bullard as his bride; then William turns somewhat paranoid and retreats to his study again. When Mandy and her child arrive, William's gruff and not especially likable sister Jane says sardonically that she knows how to take care of the baby because she has done it all her life! As soon as the reader learns that something had begun to bother Colonel Bullard a few months after Mandy arrived, the identity of Mandy's lover is for all practical purposes no longer a secret. But Harris allows five years to pass (happily in only one time-compressing chapter) before the community discovers the truth. He also drags a red herring of sorts across the plotline by having the Bullards' five-year-old son kidnapped — as it turns out by Mandy's brother, who seeks to avenge the wrong done to his sister by the Colonel. Despite the novel's structural weaknesses, Harris has succeeded by the end of the book in creating a gallery of entertaining and believable minor characters to flesh out his tale: wise old Grandsir Johnny Roach, who also appears in "Blue Dave"; Free Betsey the fortune-teller; and droll Jincy Meadows, who will become Mandy's loyal husband, are the most successful of these. True to form, Harris identifies strongly with these common people; and, as Cousins observes, he has a more difficult time giving life to the aristocratic Colonel and Mrs. Bullard. The book closes with the promise of a new moral or emotional life for several pairs of characters: the Bullards, Jincy and Mandy, and Mary and William Wornum, who has decided to come out of hiding, to try to live in the world, and to start this life with a long-overdue marriage. Yet the optimistic conclusion of the novel, as Flusche points out, only partially masks the psychological aberrations and flawed personal relationships that constitute the book's real texture.[5] As is the case in so many of his works, Harris's own anxiety and insecurity are inextricably bound up in his writing.

IV The Chronicles of Aunt Minervy Ann *(1899)*

Harris's third piece of extended narrative, *The Chronicles of Aunt Minervy Ann,* is technically not a novel but a series of inter-locked sketches written for individual publication in *Scribner's.* Comparable to his technique in "Mingo," Aunt Minervy relates her adventures to a first-person narrator, whose comments provide the linking framework for the series. As we noted in Chapter 2, Harris wrote his editor that he was more "intensely absorbed" in the Minervy Ann chronicles than in "anything I have ever written," and his own vigor and delight in his work is reflected in old Minervy's energetic personality. Her experiences as a black woman in the Reconstruction South who is making her presence felt among the whites, while she is stirring up her more reticent or lackadaisical black brethren, might better be termed escapades; for Harris's humor even verges on the slapstick in places. Nonetheless, the sketches are also characterized by the psychological and social realism that Harris usually brought to his writing. Like Uncle Remus, Aunt Minervy Ann is a "human syndicate" of several black women Harris had known. The difference in the setting of Remus's tales, the Old South plantation, and that of Minervy's, a town of average size in Middle Georgia immediately after the Civil War, helps account for the old woman's more vivid personality and aggressive behavior.

Minervy Ann declares herself to be " 'Affikin fum 'way back yander 'fo' de flood, an' fum de word go.' "[6] Strong-tempered, obstinate, and proud of her African origins, Minervy lets no man, black or white, order her life for her — especially after freedom comes. Like most of Harris's important black characters, however, Minervy is warm, generous, and loyal to those whites she does respect, including her former master, Major Tumlin Perdue. Minervy lets common sense and a basic notion of fair play govern most of her actions. Thus when her husband, Hamp, is elected a black Republican legislator, Minervy tries to warn him about becoming the tool of carpetbag politicians. She is furious when she finds out that Hamp is drawing nine dollars a day during the legislative session and spending it escorting two mulatto girls around Atlanta. Surprising him on the streets when he has his girl friends in tow, Minervy jabs Hamp in the back with her parasol, which causes him to put the lighted end of his cigar into his mouth. She then personally takes charge of an important bill that Hamp would not support and gets it passed, but she does so only after berating the legislators for their irresponsibility and laziness.

Minervy displays both her will and her physical courage in two humorous episodes. "How She Went into Business" finds the enterprising woman selling ginger-cakes and chicken pies on the Halcyondale square. Her goods are quickly bought, and she has reserved one pie for the Perdues when irascible old Salem Birch, who had been indulging his thirst earlier that afternoon, insists on buying it. At this point, Minervy Ann abruptly suspends her narrative to protest about the way people name their children: " '*Salem Birch!* Hit bangs my time how some folks kin go on — an' I ain't nothin' but a nigger. Dey's mo' chillun ruint by der names, suh, dan any udder way. I done notice et. Name one un um a Bible name, an' look like he bleedze ter go wrong. Name one un um atter some high an' mighty man, an' dey grows up wid des 'bout much sense ez a gate-post. I done watch um, suh.' '' Aunt Minervy steadfastly refuses to sell her last pie; and, when old Salem tries to take it from her, the two struggle and fall to the ground, Salem uppermost. Unflappable Minervy hollers for Major Perdue while cursing Birch; and, just as he starts to strike her, the major runs up and pulls him off the old woman.

In the other incident, which Minervy also narrates vividly and dramatically, the old lady helped Perdue fight the three Gossett boys, white trash whose father held a grudge against the Major, and who had also appeared in the two *Aaron* volumes. While Perdue wrestled with John Henry Gossett, Minervy caught Rube by the elbows and forced him down a short incline and head-over-heels into some brier bushes. She then hit Sam Gossett on the burr of the ear with a hefty rock: '' 'Twa'n't no light lick, suh; I wuz plum venomous by den; an' he went down des like a beef does when you knock 'im in de head wid a ax.' '' The Gossetts promptly called a truce.

Although Harris obviously enjoyed putting to humorous use his heroine's temper and her love of a good fight, whether verbal or physical, he also portrayed her more thoughtful and somber moments. Minervy realizes that she is viewed as a ''white folks' nigger'' because of her continuing loyalty to the Perdues, but she insists on the right to make her own decisions about for whom, or what, she will work. In ''The Case of Mary Ellen'' Minervy Ann proudly tells the story of the ''passing'' of a talented mulatto girl, who attended a Northeastern college; it is obvious that Minervy respects the cultural ideals of white society.

Perhaps the old woman's most endearing quality is her candor — and her desire that others be as honest as she. This trait is well illustrated when Minervy pays a surprise visit to the narrator's home in Atlanta and finds his wife, a Northerner, inefficiently trying to prepare dinner. Minervy Ann orders her out of the kitchen, tells her she has no more business there than a newborn baby, and proceeds to cook the meal. Later, when the conversation turns to the attitudes of ''Northrons,'' as Minervy calls them, toward ''Southrons,'' the old black woman says she knows that Northrons are mighty fine folks and that they say they are sorry for the Negroes. '' 'But I'll tell um all anywhar, any day, dat I'd lots druther dey'd be good ter me dan ter be sorry fer me.' ''

V   On the Wing of Occasions: Being the Authorised Version
of Certain Curious Episodes of the Late Civil War,
Including the Hitherto Suppressed Narrative of the
Kidnapping of President Lincoln *(1900)*

The Civil War tales in *Free Joe* and in *Tales of the Home Folks*
were, for the most part, unresearched, impressionistic glimpses of
certain phases of the struggle. Harris's lack of battle experience and
his superficial understanding of military history are also apparent
in the five tales about the Confederate secret service that comprise
On the Wing of Occasions. He does, however, achieve an esthetic
and even a philosophical unity of sorts by using the same major
characters throughout the series and by informing the tales with the
theme of providential order. In effect, then, *On the Wing of Occasions* is both a war chronicle and an extended essay on the ironic
interplay betwen men and their fate during wartime. By invoking
Providence, furthermore, Harris appealed especially to readers
below the Mason-Dixon line who rationalized that the Union's victory was somehow arranged by God.

"Why the Confederacy Failed" introduces two characters who
play central roles in the first four tales: Captain Fontaine Flournoy,
a Southern spy operating in New York City, and the Northern-born
Captain Lawrence McCarthy, another Confederate agent.
Flournoy registers at the New York Hotel, obtains secret documents containing information about Sherman's march south, and
thanks to McCarthy's help and to a little play-acting of his own,
escapes capture and travels toward Richmond with his important
dispatch. But a quirk of fate causes his mission to fail (and the
South to lose the Civil War, Harris suggests somewhat whimsi-
cally). When Flournoy thinks he is about to be captured, he gives
his dispatch to a scout and instructs him to ride on ahead. Flournoy
only encounters a party of Rebel soldiers, however, but the scout is
killed within a mile by a stray bullet; the secret document is later
used only to light a Yankee's pipe.

"The Whims of Captain McCarthy" is a slight humorous sketch
that relates how the Confederate agent effectively silenced two
Northern security officers who threatened to expose his spy operation. "In the Order of Providence" and "The Troubles of Martin
Coy" are somewhat more ambitious. Though set in Rockville

shortly after the war, both stories draw on wartime incidents for their theme. Southerners reacted to the shock of war and defeat in various ways, Harris writes in "In the Order of Providence": some died of despair, some lived on in a dream, and others went into a self-imposed exile, as was the case with Fontaine Flournoy. He made a considerable fortune as an adventurer in South America after the war, but he caught a tropical disease and returned to Middle Georgia to die. Flournoy provided well for his family and also left a handsome estate to Lawrence McCarthy, who moved to Rockville with his daughter; the two McCarthys soon were quite popular figures in town.

McCarthy's war experiences had made him an inveterate believer in the strange workings of Providence, and he especially enjoyed telling how John Omohundro, or "Texas Jack," as he was more famously known after the war,[7] had come within an ace of preventing Lincoln's assassination. Omohundro, who respected Lincoln, knew John Wilkes Booth and realized that the young actor was nervous and unbalanced in the early days of April 1865. When Booth began to rave about doing away with tyrants, Omohundro, on McCarthy's advice, locked him in his room on Good Friday afternoon. But Booth escaped by crawling out the transom and shot Lincoln that evening.

In "The Troubles of Martin Coy," Harris uses a less sensational plot, but coincidence is still his major motif. Martin Coy had fought for the South but his brother Harvey had deserted Middle Georgia for the Union cause. During a retreat through the West Virginia mountains, Martin had accidentally shot Harvey and was deeply depressed afterwards; and he also hid his face from man and from the sun — exactly as a prophecy he had heard years earlier had said he would. Martin led an ascetic life and roamed the Rockville neighborhood at night, which gave rise to various legends about "Coy's Ghost." In yet another variation on his reconciliation-through-marriage theme, Harris arranges for Martin to attend the wedding of Flournoy's son and McCarthy's daughter; to the surprise of everyone except Captain McCarthy, who had discovered his whereabouts, Harvey Coy also appears at the wedding. He had only been wounded, as it developed, but had avoided returning home because he believed Middle Georgia would not welcome him back. Martin's burden of guilt is lifted, and he always maintained during his later years that no one knew what happiness was unless they had had " 'a whole passel of trouble.' "

The most popular of the stories in *On the Wing of Occasions* was the novelette *The Kidnapping of President Lincoln,* which was chronologically the first of Harris's works to feature down-home Billy Sanders. As Franklin J. Meine suggests, Sanders is both a familiar figure in Southern literature and a unique character. He is in the main stream of Old South rural humorists — mischievous, graphic, and gifted with horse sense and storytelling ability. Yet his vitality, insight, and sympathy for humanity make him a more complex and a more likable figure than, for example, Sut Lovingood.[8] The plot of Harris's story is somewhat contrived,[9] but the delightful byplay between Sanders and Abe Lincoln, another rural philosopher famous for his love of humorous anecdotes, compensates for the structural weaknesses.

Along with young Lieutenant Francis Bethune, sixty-year-old Private Billy Sanders is sent to Washington in 1863 ostensibly to pick up a captured woman spy, whom Lincoln has generously decided to return to the Confederates instead of executing. But the secret mission of Sanders and Bethune is to kidnap Lincoln in order to stop the war. After several escapades the two men are brought to Lincoln's private room, and they soon become so impressed by Abe's humanity, wisdom, and sense of humor that their kidnapping plot loses its appeal. When Abe laughs heartily at Sanders's Cracker anecdotes and is impressed by his skill in sizing up both people and politics, Lincoln notes that it is " 'a joyous relief to meet a man who knows how to say things, and who doesn't want a post-office for himself, or his wife's cousin.' "

Harris introduces a little tension at the end of his tale by giving Billy and Francis the opportunity, during a carriage-ride with Lincoln, to fulfill their plot; however, the providential appearance of a troop of federal cavalry and their own continuing admiration for Lincoln prevent them from carrying out their plans. The story closes with Lincoln's fervent wish for peace and for the restoration of the Union, but Providence decreed that more blood would have to be shed before his hopes could be realized.

VI Gabriel Tolliver: A Story of Reconstruction *(1902)*

Gabriel Tolliver, Harris's most ambitious novel, is marred by wordiness and by the compositional problems that usually accompanied his attempts at extended narrative; but the book is a perceptive study of the South during the uncertain days of Reconstruction. In accordance with his democratic upbringing, Harris sought to portray fairly the attitudes of the Southern conservative, the more liberal Northerner, and the black people caught between the old plantation era and the new economic and political forces at work in the postwar South.

Harris wrote his novel out of a period in his own life that was rich with experience, for during the late 1860s and early 1870s he had held a series of newspaper jobs in Macon, Forsyth, and Savannah and had necessarily encountered widely divided opinion about the future of the black man in the South. He also chose a narrative persona that would give him ample opportunity to draw upon his own experiences and, at the same time, articulate his social and moral philosophy. Harris's narrator is a middle-aged author known simply as "Cephas," whose wife has persuaded him to write a book about the kind of people he knew as a lad in Shady Dale, Middle Georgia. So the narrator goes back a quarter-century to a period just after the Civil War and writes an omniscient narrative about the experiences of his young lawyer friend, Gabriel Tolliver. The boy Cephas plays only a supporting role in the tale. Freckled, short of stature, and given to blushing and self-consciousness, Cephas is obviously another ironic Harris portrait of the William Wornum mold; and the autobiographical connection becomes even more apparent if we know that Cephas, short for Josephus, was Essie Harris's nickname for her husband.

The basic plot of the book in effect summarizes Harris's thesis. The villain in the novel, Gilbert Hotchkiss, is an overly zealous, manipulative carpetbagger who tries to radicalize the "niggeroes" of Shady Dale. When Hotchkiss is killed by a black man who thinks that the carpetbagger has been making a play for his wife, the blame for the murder temporarily falls upon Gabriel Tolliver. However, Gabriel is rescued from the federal guards by Billy Sanders, Cephas, and other friends, who keep him under cover until the case against him is dropped. At the end of the book, Gabriel gives a speech that expresses Harris's constant theme of reconciliation and understanding between North and South. Gabriel, a spokesman for the artist, represents the new breed of Southerner who looks to a brighter era of mutual respect and of political and economic progress in a war-torn land. Tolliver, like Harris, scorns extremism in any form, seeking moderation instead.

Various subplots and reconciled or maturing love relationships counterpoint Harris's dominant theme of charity over hatred and of mutuality over divisiveness. Yet again, Harris may too easily mend relationships or resolve personality conflicts. Cephas remains an unattractive and insecure figure, despite his generous support of Gabriel. Or, to use an example that Flusche cites, Margaret Gaither's rejuvenated love for Pulaski Tumlin does not eradicate in the reader's mind the reason for her abandoning her intended in the first place: the side of his face had been badly burned when he saved his sister from a fire, and for years Margaret could not bear to look at him. Harris was apparently constitutionally incapable of portraying human relationships that began and ended normally.

Harris's dialect portraits in *Gabriel Tolliver* are brilliant, but the real strength of his Reconstruction tale lies in his depiction of the restlessness, uneasiness, and strange silence pervasive among the blacks who are trying to come to grips with their new freedom after the war. Gabriel sees their restlessness as natural, but many of his elders in the community interpret it as the harbinger of violent rebellion or revenge-taking. When carpetbaggers calling themselves Republicans and radical Union League reformers from the North begin to infiltrate the black settlements, the whites grow even more nervous. Loyal and conservative blacks like old Uncle Plato are not convinced by the carpetbagger claim that the Southern whites are only planning to reenslave them. Yet Reverend Jeremiah Tomlin and others are temporarily persuaded by Hotchkiss's incendiary pitch that the former slaves deserve to reclaim from the whites, by force, every dollar they had been compelled to earn for their masters.

Gabriel and the more thoughtful whites in Shady Dale realized that state politics were growing more manipulative and corrupt under the influence of carpetbaggers like Hotchkiss, who would do their best to keep qualified Southern leadership out of the state house. One group of angry whites, who wore white hoods and called themselves the Knights of the White Camellia, tried to disrupt Hotchkiss's organizing activities at Reverend Jeremiah's church by riding their horses around the yard and pursuing the terrified old minister down the road. Harris resolves this incident too easily by claiming that the White Camellias were not so radical as the Ku Klux Klan and that Jeremiah laughed at the occurrence in his later years. Almost in spite of himself, however, Harris again reveals an important component of the Southern consciousness: the propensity for violence among those whites who found the defeat experience of the war and their own loss of property or position ironically mocked by the black man, whose rise to power seemed to presage yet another defeat for the white man.

Tensions in Shady Dale are high, but the community finds a type of catharsis when Hotchkiss is shot while talking with the flirtatious high-yellow wife of Ike Varner, a happy-go-lucky Negro whose only vice has been his jealousy about his Edie. Gabriel is implicated at first because Hotchkiss had his name on his lips when he died, but Harris leaves little doubt that Ike had shot Hotchkiss. It is ironic that the carpetbagger was totally innocent of any involvement with Edie and that Ike, the murderer, flees the county and is never prosecuted. Either Harris grew careless, or his social and racial vision conveniently merged with his sense of morality: he implies that an ignorant Negro could not be blamed for a crime of passion committed against an unprincipled carpetbagger.

VII *The Late Novels (1904–1907)*

Harris published as magazine serials three short novels during the closing years of his life, and the most entertaining of these were two Civil War adventures, *A Little Union Scout* (1904) and *The Shadow Between His Shoulder-Blades,* a Billy Sanders narrative printed in book form in 1909. *The Bishop and the Boogerman,* also published as a complete volume in 1909, is ostensibly an adolescent novel; but Harris's use of Billy Sanders as town sage and his introduction of adult themes imply a more mature audience; however, the tale suffers because of Harris's lack of authorial focus. Set in 1868, it tells how a young girl and Billy Sanders befriend a black man who had knocked a cruel overseer on the head in 1864 and had ever since been in hiding. The former slave's fate remains tenuous for a period while Sanders helps resolve a complicated legal issue. Late in the story Harris abruptly introduces a secondary plot, a love story, that gives the Sage of Shady Dale other chances to reveal both his humanity and his horse sense.

A Little Union Scout, an episodic adventure tale, proved very popular in Harris's day; but it relies too heavily upon romantic coincidence for most modern readers. At the request of an inquisitive college girl, the first-person narrator recounts his experiences fighting with General Nathan Forrest's brigade against federal troops in Alabama and Tennessee. Coincidentally, while the narrator is keeping his eye on some would-be horse thieves, he finds documents intended for Frank Leroy, a famous Union scout. He soon realizes that Frank Leroy is in reality Miss Jane Ryder, an attractive young girl whom the narrator begins to fall in love with despite her anti-Secessionist viewpoint. Following a series of adventures, and further coincidences, the two young people agree to meet a year after the war is over; and another marriage between North and South is the inevitable result. " 'Ain't war a hell of a thing?' " asks an old lady who is caring for a wounded soldier early in the novelette. Yet in this book Harris begs his own question and chooses to emphasize the romance over the reality of war.

In the next novel, however, Harris's perspective is notably different. While Billy Sanders's sardonic sense of humor and marvelous expository narrative style make *The Shadow Between His Shoulder-Blades* one of Harris's best war stories, the tale is even more appealing because it undercuts wartime heroics and shows the absurdity and confusion that often attend battle. Shady Dale's village scion enjoys sitting on the veranda of the local tavern and sharing stories as well as pet peeves with all listeners in range. Billy usually manages to fire off a few salvoes at big plantation owners and at uppity Negroes before he turns to his favorite subject, his war experiences. Wimberly Driscoll, one of Billy's best friends, had lost a foot in the war about the same time Billy caught a bullet in the stomach; but Billy cannot let Wimberly's close-fisted manner of running his plantation after the war remain uncommented upon. Wimberly " 'runs his farm wi' a club an' the multiplication table, an' you can't git his han's away from 'im for love nor money. He's got ever'thing screwed up so tight that ef a spring was to break the whole county'd be kivvered wi' meat an' wheat an' lint cotton.' "

And Wimberly's old Mammy Kitty, who served the family during the war, was a ferocious creature when she was roused. After a period of recuperation, Sanders came to take his friend back to the battlefield, but Mammy Kitty refused to let him go. Sanders tells his mixed crowd of listeners: " 'He had n't more'n got on the gray mar' before ol' Kitty opened up, an' she preached his funer'l, an' she preached it at the top of her voice. Ef one of you Northern fellers could 'a' heern 'er, you'd 'a' got a bran' new idee in regards to the oppressed colored people.' "

When Billy talks about the war, he admits that in the latter days of the struggle he had grown pretty well soured on the so-called glory of battle. " 'You may think it mighty funny, but, when a man's been to war, somethin' nice goes out'n him; he ain't the same; he gits oneasy, an' the Ol' Boy creeps up an' grips him in the neighborhood of his thinkin' machine. It's took me these many long years for to git rid of the feelin'.' '' Two particular episodes had helped bring Sanders to this point of view. The first demonstrated to him the absurdity of battle, and the second had a frightening psychological effect because it revealed how arbitrary and treacherous war could become. In the first incident, Sanders and his lame companion Driscoll alone rout four Union cavalrymen and take two prisoners merely by spurring their horses into the midst of the Yankee patrol. Sanders realized how absurd battle could be when, amidst the general confusion, he heard one Yankee complain, " 'Don't you know if you drag me off'n this hoss I'll git hurt?' " To add to the irony of the whole episode, General Forrest later praises the two men for their masterful surprise tactics.

In the second incident, Billy saw something of the horror of war when he and Driscoll were betrayed by a spy into Union hands. The two were jailed in Murphreesboro and were awaiting execution when Forrest raided the town, but the spy set the jail on fire just before the Confederate troops arrived to release them. Billy never forgot those last frightening moments in the flames. When the spy was caught and hanged by Forrest, Sanders had another image etched on his memory, for he realized how close he had come to the same fate. For days and days, he explains, " 'I could feel the shadder of that black, swingin' thing right betwixt my shoulder-blades; an' when I'm off in my feed I can feel it yit; sometimes it's cold, sometimes it's hot.' " Harris may have had his difficulties in sustaining a plot across an extended narrative, but he was a master of the vignette of character and scene.

CHAPTER 7

Harris in Perspective

BOTH in his writings and in his personal life Joel Chandler Harris remains a contradictory figure. It is apparent that the tensions and psychological stresses he felt during his career made him a better writer, and so we are glad, for posterity's sake, that Harris's was not a more "normal" personality. Had he been secure and confident in his work as one of the nation's leading journalists, he might not have kept harking back to those nostalgic and essentially trouble-free years at Turnwold Plantation, and he consequently might not have written the Uncle Remus books and the other works that followed them. The split between Harris's public and private self in effect left America with two literary heritages rather than just one. As a talented columnist and the leading editorial-writer for the *Constitution,* one of the most prestigious newspapers in the country, Harris would clearly have left his mark on American Reconstruction and post-Reconstruction history, anyhow. But, as the author of *Uncle Remus,* "Free Joe," "Mingo," and other works, Harris achieved an international reputation among an incredibly varied audience of readers: professional folklorists, social historians, authors and critics, political and industrial leaders, psychologists, and the great range of common readers, including the children.

Among the several tensions and contradictions in Harris's writing, the healthiest is that between the universal and the particular. Harris's works treat the broad humanistic and social themes that are part of the history of mankind; and, because of his instinctive feel for the humorous and ironic possibilities in human behavior, *Uncle Remus* has become one of the world's most widely translated literary works, now available in over twenty foreign-language editions. Harris's celebrated use of reverse psychology in the tar-baby

145

story has made being thrown into the brier patch an internationally recognized metaphor. Harris has been cited in British House of Commons debates and in *Newsweek* essays about interstate commerce deregulation. Among the many popular-culture heirs of Brer Rabbit and Brer Fox are the Road Runner and the Coyote, Tom and Jerry, Tweetie and Sylvester, a gallery of Disney animal characters, and Bugs Bunny and his various rivals from the Tasmanian Devil to Elmer Fudd. Fudd may be a variation of Mr. Man in the Remus tales, and Bugs Bunny's impertinent "Eh, what's up, Doc?" is in effect a reworking of Brer Rabbit's "How duz yo' sym'tums seem ter segashuate?"

But it is Harris's keen perception of the particulars of language and human psychology that continues to impress scholars and critics. Harris's own supersensitive nature made him acutely aware of the subtle gestures, glances, and innuendoes that often convey enormous meanings. Uncle Remus, Billy Sanders, Aunt Minervy Ann, and Mingo are vital and enduring characters because they themselves are accomplished narrative artists and students of human nature who bring us easily into their world and let us walk around in it with them. In 1926, four hundred teachers of high-school and college literature ranked *Uncle Remus* fifth among works of American literature that deserved international stature. The first four places were held by Poe's *Tales,* Nathaniel Hawthorne's *The Scarlet Letter,* Twain's *Huckleberry Finn,* and Cooper's *The Last of the Mohicans;* and the novel in the sixth position was Melville's *Moby-Dick.*[1] Linguists and folklorists have become even more impressed over the years by Harris's discerning ear for speech patterns and his eye for the details of folk tradition; for, in making his incredibly precise transcriptions of the speech, gestures, and folk beliefs of an era and its peoples, he produced an anthropological and linguistic profile that would otherwise be unobtainable.

Another contradiction in Harris is implied in the dichotomies of which I have just spoken: Harris was a popular author, but he was also a literary artist. Having as a basis for his writing the oral tradition of the people, and identifying as strongly as he did with the common folk, Harris knew how to tell a story that the people would like. As a journalist, furthermore, he realized the propagandistic value of literature; and he consciously shaped his tales to help heal the wounds that the Civil War had produced on both sides of the Mason-Dixon line. Reconciliation, mutual acceptance, love and marriage, Northerners comfortably at home in the South, and the happy resolution of personal conflicts were Harris's official, public themes. The signs are that his stories did, in fact, help bring the North and the South closer together during the uncertain years after the war.

Yet deeper readers and critics have found the texture of Harris's writing to be much more sophisticated and complex than its often humorous or facile surface suggests. Even in the early Remus books Harris employed imagery symbolically and gave his old narrator subtle psychological and rhetorical techniques to use as leverage on his young listener. The question of the final meaning of the Remus tales, moreover, continues to intrigue literary and social critics, and even black writers cannot agree about Harris's depth of penetration into the Negro mind. I believe, however, that Harris demonstrated more insight into the black consciousness than any white author prior to Mark Twain and that he created a more complete and authentically portrayed cast of black characters than any writer of the nineteenth century.

In the short fiction — which is Harris's most accomplished writing and deserves more recognition — and also in the novels, Harris broadened his range of characters, his settings, and his psychological themes. As an expository author steeped in the oral tradition, Harris tended to write leisurely and loose narratives, but the gain in dialect portraiture and in close attention to character psychology is worth any loss in momentum or form. To be sure, Harris occasionally settled for the stereotypical when he might have worked for greater originality, and at times his notion of pathos could more accurately be termed excessive sentimentality. Nonetheless, no author of Harris's day surpassed his sensitivity to the condition and personality traits of the poor white and to the nature of the black experience.

In his oft-cited and only slightly overstated essay of 1888, "The South as a Field for Fiction," Albion Tourgée claimed that Southern literature had already become synonymous with American literature and that the Negro as a man, and not as a slave, was the richest mine of material available to the serious author.[2] Harris's writings helped to bring both Southern literature and the black character into the mainstream of the nation's art, and considerable evidence exists that Twain and Faulkner owe a greater debt to Harris than to any other predecessor in the field of Southern letters. Uncle Remus's relationship to the little boy and the force of character, insight, and powers of endurance displayed by Mingo, Minervy Ann, Uncle Remus, and other black figures are patterns that find close analogues in *Huckleberry Finn,* and in *Absalom, Absalom!, The Sound and the Fury,* and *Go Down, Moses.* Indeed, the ultimate influence of Joel Chandler Harris on American literature has yet to be fully appraised.

Harris inevitably brought his own psychological tensions and contradictions to his writing, and his portraits of the artist appear, under various guises and surrogates, in one story and novel after another. To the end of his life he remained a deeply insecure man; his attempts to find a viable identity for himself in his fiction-writing and to achieve some sort of catharsis of his self-consciousness and feelings of inadequacy were never successful. In filling out a questionnaire for *Book-Buyer* magazine in 1893, Harris wrote tellingly that what he most detested were applications for autographs and that what he most admired in men was modesty. When asked what "gift of nature" he should most like to have, Harris wrote "The Gift of Gab"[3]; and a whole life of torment was involved in that one response.

Harris found at least some therapeutic value in his writing and in his participation in public life, but his well-cultivated sense of humor was probably his greatest psychological asset. He lived by it, it informed some of his best writing, and he died by it. His humorous sensibility left American literature with one of its most important legacies in the comic imagination, and it also gave Harris's contradictory and anxiety-filled life the only wholeness he would ever know.

Notes and References

Note: Unless otherwise indicated, quotations from Harris's works are drawn from the editions cited in Chapters 1 and 2.

Preface

1. Robert L. Wiggins, *The Life of Joel Chandler Harris: From Obscurity in Boyhood to Fame in Early Manhood* (Nashville, Dallas, Richmond, 1918).

2. Julia Collier Harris, *The Life and Letters of Joel Chandler Harris* (Boston and New York, 1918).

3. Paul Cousins, *Joel Chandler Harris: A Biography* (Baton Rouge, La., 1968).

4. Joseph M. Griska, Jr., of Houston Baptist University is currently preparing a scholarly edition of Harris's letters.

5. Stella Brewer Brookes, *Joel Chandler Harris — Folklorist* (Athens, Ga., 1950).

6. Julia Collier Harris, *Joel Chandler Harris: Editor and Essayist* (Chapel Hill, N.C., 1931).

Chapter One

1. In "An Accidental Author," a brief autobiographical sketch written for *Lippincott's* XXXVII (April 1886), pp. 417-20, Harris mentioned that he was born "in the humblest sort of circumstances." Harris's letters to Mrs. Georgia Starke constitute some of his most intimate self-portraits; yet in the most direct reference to his origins that has been published he only notes that his history was "a peculiarly sad and unfortunate one" (letter of December 9, 1870, in Harris, *Life and Letters,* p. 78).

2. Letter of May 6, 1891, Duke University Harris Collection.

3. In this study, I have drawn especially upon the following discussions of the relationship between Harris's complex personality and his career: Jay Martin, *Harvests of Change: American Literature 1865-1914* (Englewood Cliffs, N.J., 1967), pp. 96-98; Louis D. Rubin, Jr., "Uncle Remus and the Ubiquitous Rabbit,, *Southern Review,* NS X (October

1974), pp. 784–804; Michael Flusche, "Underlying Despair in the Fiction of Joel Chandler Harris," *Mississippi Quarterly,* XXIX (Winter 1975–76), pp. 91–103.

4. Cousins, *Harris,* pp. 3–21.

5. See particularly A. B. Longstreet's *Georgia Scenes, Characters, and Incidents* (1835); W. T. Thompson's *Major Jones's Courtship* (1843); C. H. Smith's *Bill Arp, So-Called, A Side Show of the Southern Side of the War* (1866); and R. M. Johnston's *Dukesborough Tales* (1871).

6. Cousins, *Harris,* p. 24.

7. [F. W. Halsey], "Joel Chandler Harris," *New York Times Saturday Review,* December 28, 1901, p. 1016.

8. So Harris's persona terms himself in *Gabriel Tolliver: A Story of Reconstruction* (New York, 1902), p. 353.

9. Harris, "Humor in America," introduction to *American Wit and Humor: by One Hundred of America's Leading Humorists* (New York, 1907), IV, pp. xx–xxi.

10. Cousins, *Harris,* p. 35.

11. *On the Plantation: A Story of a Georgia Boy's Adventures During the War* (New York, 1892), chapters four, seven, and twelve.

12. Cousins, *Harris,* pp. 60–61.

13. Quoted in Wiggins, *Harris,* p. 156.

14. See Thomas H. English, "Joel Chandler Harris's Earliest Literary Project," *Emory University Quarterly,* II (October 1946), pp. 176–85.

15. Jay B. Hubbell, *Southern Life in Fiction* (Athens, Ga., 1960), p. 82.

16. Quoted in Harris, *Life and Letters,* p. 63.

17. *Ibid.,* pp. 83, 85.

18. Wiggins, *Harris,* p. 88.

19. See Harris, *Editor and Essayist,* pp. 6, 9.

20. Julian LaRose (b. 1874), Lucien (1875), Evan Howell (1876), Evelyn (1878), Mary Esther (1879), Lillian (1882), Linton (1883), Mildred (1885), and Joel Chandler, Jr. (1888). Evan Howell died in 1878 after a measles attack; Mary Esther and Linton died of diptheria in 1882 and 1890, respectively. Julian Harris was awarded a Pulitzer Prize in 1926 for his investigation of Ku Klux Klan activities and for other aggressive journalism. As editor of the Columbus, Georgia, *Enquirer Sun,* Julian, the prize statement reads, waged a "brave and energetic fight against the KKK; against the enactment of a law barring the teaching of evolution; against dishonest and incompetent public officials and for justice to the negro and against lynching" (the plaque is displayed in the Harris Room at Emory). For an account of Julian's career and the influence of his father upon it, see William F. Mugleston, "Julian Harris, the Georgia Press, and the Ku Klux Klan," *Georgia Historical Quarterly,* LIX (Fall 1975), pp. 284–95, and John M. Matthews, "Julian L. Harris: The Evolution of a Southern Liberal," *South Atlantic Quarterly,* LXXV (Autumn 1976), 483–98.

21. These figures are drawn from the eighth, ninth, and tenth censuses of the United States. Nashville, Tennessee, was Atlanta's closest rival in postwar growth rate.

22. Cousins, *Harris,* p. 96.

23. Twain, "How to Tell a Story," in *How to Tell a Story and Other Essays* (New York and London, 1905), pp. 3–9 *passim.*

24. Harris, *Life and Letters,* pp. 146 and 146 n.1.

25. Thomas H. English, "The Twice-Told Tale and Uncle Remus," *Georgia Review,* II (Winter 1948), p. 452, and "The Other Uncle Remus," *Georgia Review,* XXI (Summer 1967), pp. 210–17.

26. Thomas H. English, "Fun in a Newspaper Office," *Ex Libris: An Occasional Publication of the Friends of the Emory University Library,* XIV (June 1975), pp. 8–10.

27. Quoted in Harris, *Editor and Essayist,* p. 38.

28. For a careful study of Harris's social views, see Herndon's unpublished dissertation, "Social Comment in the Writings of Joel Chandler Harris," Duke University, 1966.

29. James C. Derby, *Fifty Years Among Authors, Books and Publishers* (New York, 1884), p. 434.

30. Cousins, *Harris,* p. 113.

31. For a full account of Harris's relationship to his illustrators, see Beverly R. David, "Visions of the South: Joel Chandler Harris and His Illustrators," *American Literary Realism,* IX (Summer 1976), pp. 189–206.

32. Walter Hines Page, "The New South," *Boston Post,* September 28, 1881.

33. I am indebted to Joseph Griska for alerting me to this letter, which is among Duke University's Harris papers.

Chapter Two

1. Harris, *Life and Letters,* p. 168.

2. For Twain's letters to Harris during this period and explanatory notes, see Thomas H. English, ed., *Mark Twain to Uncle Remus 1881–1885* (Atlanta, 1953).

3. Arlin Turner, *George W. Cable* (Baton Rouge, La., 1966), p. 121.

4. See Twain's letter to W. D. Howells of February 27, 1881, in Albert Bigelow Paine, ed., *Mark Twain's Letters* (New York, 1917), I, p. 395.

5. Mark Twain, *Life on the Mississippi* (Boston, 1883), pp. 471–72.

6. In a letter to Appleton's shortly afterwards (quoted in Cousins, *Harris,* p. 126).

7. See Joseph M. Griska, Jr., "Two New Joel Chandler Harris Reviews of Mark Twain," *American Literature,* XLVIII (January 1977), pp. 584–89. The reviews were published on June 11, 1882, and May 26, 1885.

8. See Turner, *George W. Cable,* pp. 232–33, and Harris, *Life and Letters,* pp. 207–209.

9. Grady's speech is reproduced in *Joel Chandler Harris' Life of Henry W. Grady* (New York, 1890), pp. 83–93.

10. See *Joel Chandler Harris' Life of Henry W. Grady,* pp. 9–68, and Raymond B. Nixon's biography, *Henry W. Grady: Spokesman of the New South* (New York, 1943).

11. Charles William McCreery Johnson and Thomas H. English have carefully described and catalogued 5,854 manuscript pages in the Harris Collection at Emory University. The evidence is that Harris wrote most of the Remus stories straight out, but the local-color stories and novels that come later were often revised; one short story manuscript contains fifteen false starts, for example. Some stories are restructured, and in other places Harris rejects as many as a dozen pages from a tale.

12. An important study of Harris's working relationships with editors Gilder and Robert Underwood Johnson is Herbert F. Smith's "Joel Chandler Harris's Contributions to *Scribner's Monthly* and *Century Magazine,*" *Georgia Historical Quarterly,* XLVII (June 1963), pp. 169–79.

13. See also Henry M. Reed, *The A. B. Frost Book* (Rutland, Vt., 1967), pp. 59–68, and David, "Visions of the South: Joel Chandler Harris and His Illustrators," cited in Chapter 1.

14. A useful assessment of Russell's work is G. William Nott's "Irwin Russell, First Dialect Author," *Southern Literary Messenger,* I (December 1939), pp. 809–14.

15. *Daddy Jake, the Runaway, and Short Stories Told After Dark* (New York, 1889).

16. *Balaam and His Master and Other Sketches and Stories* (Boston and New York, 1891).

17. *On the Plantation: A Story of a Georgia Boy's Adventures During the War,* cited in Chapter 1.

18. *Uncle Remus and His Friends* (Boston and New York, 1892).

19. *Evening Tales* (New York, 1893).

20. *Georgia from the Invasion of DeSoto to Recent Times* (New York, 1896) was republished the same year as *Stories of Georgia.* Harris corrected factual errors in his account of the Yankees' capture of the Confederate locomotive, "The General," before the second printing of the Appleton edition.

21. *Wally Wanderoon* was published by McClure, Phillips and Co., New York; the other volumes were released by Houghton Mifflin and Co., New York.

22. Letter to Harris of December 6, 1895, in Harris, *Life and Letters,* pp. 333–34.

23. *Sister Jane: Her Friends and Acquaintances* (Boston and New York, 1896), p. 128.

24. *Tales of the Home Folks in Peace and War* (Boston and New York, 1898).

25. In a personal copy of *Nights with Uncle Remus* that was later sold at auction, Harris wrote the following comment (no date is affixed): "The introduction is a gem. It should be read with eyes half closed in order to get the full effect of the vast learning it contains. The reader will naturally think it represents some knowledge of comparative folk-lore on the part of the author. He is willing to make an affidavit that he knows no more on the subject than a blind horse knows about Sunday" (quoted in Cousins, *Harris,* p. 130 n.39).

26. Letter of April 25, 1896, in Harris, *Life and Letters,* p. 351.

27. Letter of March 19, 1898, *op. cit.,* pp. 384–86.

28. Jay Martin, *Harvests of Change: American Literature 1865–1914,* p. 98.

29. *The Chronicles of Aunt Minervy Ann* (New York, 1899).

30. Letter of November 14, 1898, in Harris, *Life and Letters,* p. 403.

31. *On the Wing of Occasions: Being the Authorised Version of Certain Curious Episodes of the Late Civil War, Including the Hitherto Suppressed Narrative of the Kidnapping of President Lincoln* (New York, 1900).

32. See "The Farmer of Snap-Bean Farm," *Uncle Remus's The Home Magazine,* XXIV (September 1908), p. 7, and Edward Anthony's biography, *O Rare Don Marquis* (Garden Ctiy, N.Y., 1962), p. 87. For a study of Harris's influence on Marquis's writings, see Hamlin L. Hill, "Archy and Uncle Remus: Don Marquis's Debt to Joel Chandler Harris," *Georgia Review,* XV (Spring 1961), pp. 78–87.

33. *The Making of a Statesman, and Other Stories* (New York, 1902).

34. Letter of June 1, 1900, in Harris, *Life and Letters,* p. 453.

35. Thomas H. English, "Introduction," *Qua: A Romance of the Revolution* (Atlanta, 1946), p. 10.

36. *Gabriel Tolliver: A Story of Reconstruction* (New York, 1902).

37. Henry E. Harman, "Joel Chandler Harris," *Bookman,* LXI (June 1925), pp. 433–36.

38. The novel appeared in the *Saturday Evening Post* in February and March 1904 and was published in book form by McClure, Phillips and Co., New York, later that year.

39. *The Tar-Baby and Other Rhymes of Uncle Remus* (New York, 1904).

40. *Told by Uncle Remus: New Stories of the Old Plantation* (New York, 1905).

41. Arlin Turner, "Joel Chandler Harris in the Currents of Change," *Southern Literary Journal,* I (Autumn 1968), p. 110.

42. The three essays are collected in Harris, *Editor and Essayist,* pp. 114–59.

43. Margot Gayle, "Georgia's Aesop," *Holland's,* LXVII (December 1948), pp. 8–9.

44. Anonymous, "Roosevelt's Tribute to Famous Georgian," *Atlanta News,* October 21, 1905, p. 1.

45. Letter of June 28, 1917, to Julia Collier Harris in Harris, *Life and Letters,* p. 515.

46. *Ibid.,* p. 517.

47. Cousins, *Harris,* p. 209. For an account of the magazine's fortunes under Harris's and later his son Julian's editorship, see William F. Mugleston, "The Perils of Southern Publishing: a History of *Uncle Remus's Magazine,*" *Journalism Quarterly,* LII (Autumn 1975), pp. 515-21, 608. The magazine ceased publication in February 1913.

48. Initially entitled *The Bishop, The Boogerman, and the Right of Way,* the novel first appeared in serial form in the June-October 1907 numbers of *Uncle Remus's Magazine.* It was published as a book by Doubleday, Page and Co. in 1909.

49. *Uncle Remus and Brer Rabbit* (New York, 1907).

50. The novel was published as a book in 1909 by Small, Maynard and Co., Boston.

51. Harris, *Life and Letters,* p. 582.

52. *Ibid.,* p. 588.

53. *Uncle Remus and the Little Boy* (Boston, 1910).

54. *Uncle Remus Returns* (Boston and New York, 1918).

55. *The Witch Wolf* (Cambridge, Mass., 1921). This tale had been published earlier in *Daddy Jake* (1889).

56. *Seven Tales of Uncle Remus* (Atlanta, 1948).

57. From 1894 through 1920, McKinlay, Stone & MacKenzie, New York, published eleven volumes of Harris's works in a uniform edition, but no complete edition of his writing has appeared to date.

58. Cousins, *Harris,* p. 221.

Chapter Three

1. All quotations from the introduction to *Uncle Remus: His Songs and His Sayings* are from the first edition (New York, c. 1880 [publication date 1881]), pp. 3-12. Quotations from the text are from the 1974 reprinting of the 1895 Appleton edition by Grosset & Dunlap, New York.

2. See Henry A. Beers, *An Outline Sketch of American Literature* (New York, 1887), p. 268.

3. Baskervill's monograph on Harris was bound in Volume I of *Southern Writers: Biographical and Critical Studies* (Nashville, 1897), pp. 41-88. Wiggins's and Harris's biographies have been drawn upon frequently in this study.

4. See Gaines, *The Southern Plantation: A Study in the Development and the Accuracy of a Tradition* (New York, 1925), pp. 74-78, *et passim;* Blair, *Native American Humor* (New York, 1937), pp. 137-38, 143-46, *et passim;* English, "In Memory of Uncle Remus," *Southern Literary Messenger,* II (February 1940), pp. 77-83; and Hubbell, *The South in American Literature* (Durham, N.C.; 1954), pp. 782-95.

5. Ellen Douglass Leyburn, *Satiric Allegory: Mirror of Man* (New Haven, 1956), pp. 57, 60–66.

6. Wade Hall, *The Smiling Phoenix: Southern Humor from 1865 to 1914* (Gainesville, Fla., 1965), pp. 77–78, 113–14, *et passim;* and Jay Martin, *Harvests of Change: American Literature 1865–1914,* pp. 96–100. I have frequently cited Cousins's biography.

7. See David A. Walton, "Joel Chandler Harris as Folklorist: A Reassessment," *Keystone Folklore Quarterly,* XI (Spring 1966), pp. 21–26, and Michael Flusche, "Joel Chandler Harris and the Folklore of Slavery," *Journal of American Studies,* IX (December 1975), pp. 347–63. Richard M. Dorson discusses the significance of the Old Marster and John tales in *Negro Folktales in Michigan* (Cambridge, Mass., 1956), p. 49.

8. T. F. Crane, "Plantation Folk-Lore," *Popular Science Monthly,* XVIII (April 1881), pp. 824–33.

9. See particularly Charles C. Jones, Jr., *Negro Myths from the Georgia Coast: Told in the Vernacular* (Boston and New York, 1888), and A. M. H. Christensen, *Afro-American Folk Lore Told Round Cabin Fires on the Sea Islands of South Carolina* (Boston, 1892).

10. Joseph Jacobs first mentioned his theory in his introduction to *The Earliest English Version of the Fables of Bidpai* (London, 1888), pp. xliv–xlvi, and elaborated upon it in notes to *The Fables of Aesop* (1889) and *Indian Fairy Tales* (1892).

11. Aurelio M. Espinosa's first article on sources for the Brer Rabbit tales appeared in 1911; see especially "A New Classification of the Fundamental Elements of the Tar-Baby Story on the Basis of Two Hundred and Sixty-Seven Versions," *Journal of American Folk-Lore,* LVI (January-March 1943), pp. 31–37. A more general discussion is Ruth Cline's "The Tar-Baby Story," *American Literature,* II (March 1930), pp. 72–78.

12. F. M. Warren, " 'Uncle Remus' and 'The Roman de Renard,' " *Modern Language Notes,* V (May 1890), pp. 257–70; Adolf Gerber, "Uncle Remus Traced to the Old World," *Journal of American Folk-Lore,* VI (October-December 1893), pp. 245–57; W. Norman Brown, "The Tar-Baby at Home," *Scientific Monthly,* XV (September 1922), pp. 228–34, and "The Stickfast Motif in the Tar-Baby Story," *Publications of the Philadelphia Anthropological Society* (Philadelphia, Pa., 1937), I, pp. 1–12. Of E. C. Parsons's several articles on Harris's sources, see in particular "Joel Chandler Harris and Negro Folklore," *Dial,* LXVI (May 17, 1919), pp. 491–93, and "Tar Baby," *Journal of American Folk-Lore,* XXXV (July-September 1922), p. 330.

13. W. D. Piersen, "An African Background for American Negro Folktales?" *Journal of American Folklore,* LXXXIV (April-June 1971), pp. 204–14, and D. J. M. Muffett, "Uncle Remus Was a Hausaman?," *Southern Folklore Quarterly,* XXXIX (June 1975), pp. 151–66.

14. In this connection, see Michael Flusche, "Joel Chandler Harris and the Folklore of Slavery," *op. cit.*

15. G. P. Krapp, *The English Language in America* (New York, 1925), I, pp. 240–42, 248–51; II, *passim*. See also Sumner Ives, "A Theory of Literary Dialect," *Tulane Studies in English,* II (1950), pp. 137–82; *The Phonology of the Uncle Remus Tales* (Gainesville, Fla., 1954); "Dialect Differentiation in the Stories of Joel Chandler Harris," *American Literature,* XXVII (March 1955), pp. 88–96.

16. Kathleen Light, "Uncle Remus and the Folklorists," *Southern Literary Journal,* VII (Spring 1975), pp. 88–104.

17. B. A. Botkin, "Brer Rabbit," *Funk & Wagnalls Standard Dictionary of Folklore, Mythology, and Legend* (New York, 1949), I, p. 163.

18. Louise Dauner, "Myth and Humor in the Uncle Remus Fables," *American Literature,* XX (May 1948), pp. 129–43; Paul Radin, *The Trickster: A Study in American Indian Mythology* (New York, 1956), *passim;* Carl Jung's essay, "On the Psychology of the Trickster Figure," is included as an appendix in Radin's study, pp. 195–211.

19. Brookes, *Harris — Folklorist,* pp. 150–52.

20. See Roger D. Abrahams, *Deep Down in the Jungle ... Negro Narrative Folklore from the Streets of Philadelphia* (Chicago, 1970), pp. 62, 70–74, and Richard M. Dorson, *American in Legend* (New York, 1973), p. 126.

21. Sterling Brown, "Negro Character as Seen by White Authors," *Journal of Negro Education,* II (April 1933), pp. 180–97 passim. See also Brown's *The Negro in American Fiction* (Washington, D.C., 1937), pp. 53–58, and "A Century of Negro Portraiture in American Literature, *Massachusetts Review,* VII (Winter 1966), pp. 76–78.

22. Darwin T. Turner, "Daddy Joel Harris and His Old-Time Darkies," *Southern Literary Journal,* I (December 1968), pp. 20–41.

23. See Brewer's notes to *American Negro Folklore* (Chicago, 1968), pp. 3–4, 9, 28.

24. Daniel G. Hoffman, *Form and Fable in American Fiction* (New York, 1961), p. 341; and Lyle Glazier, "The Uncle Remus Stories: Two Portraits of American Negroes," *Hacettepe Bulletin of Social Sciences and Humanities,* I (June 1969), 67–74 (reprinted in *Journal of General Education,* XXII [April 1970], pp. 71–79).

25. Robert Bone, *Down Home: A History of Afro-American Short Fiction from Its Beginnings to the End of the Harlem Renaissance* (New York, 1975), pp. 13–17, 19–40.

26. Bernard Wolfe, "Uncle Remus and the Malevolent Rabbit," *Commentary, VIII (July 1949), pp. 31–41.*

27. Jesse Bier, *The Rise and Fall of American Humor* (New York, 1968), pp. 80, 81, 82, *et passim.*

28. See Flusche's essay, "Underlying Despair in the Fiction of Joel Chandler Harris," cited in Chapter 1.

29. See Louis Rubin's "Southern Local Color and The Black Man," *Southern Review,* NS VI (October 1970), pp. 1014–15, 1016–22, and

"Uncle Remus and the Ubiquitous Rabbit," cited in Chapter 1.

30. See especially Leslie Fiedler's "Come Back to the Raft Ag'in, Huck Honey!" *Partisan Review,* XV (June 1948), pp. 664–71.

31. Leyburn, *Satiric Allegory: Mirror of Man,* pp. 60, 63.

32. John Stafford, in "Patterns of Meaning in *Nights with Uncle Remus,*" *American Literature,* XVIII (May 1946), pp. 89–108, finds in Harris's second book complex and overlapping literary and mythic strategies. Harris wrote in the pastoral tradition, romanticizing the feudal Southern past but meanwhile parodying the white social structure through the antics of Jack, 'Tildy, Remus, and Tempy. Brer Rabbit serves a priestly function in the more magical-religious tales in the volume.

33. *Down Home,* pp. 19–40 *passim.*

Chapter Four

1. *Seven Tales of Uncle Remus,* cited in Chapter 2.

2. James B. Morrow, "Joel Chandler Harris Talks of Himself and Uncle Remus," *Boston Globe,* November 3, 1907.

3. Harris, *Life and Letters,* p. 321.

Chapter Five

1. Derby, *Fifty Years Among Authors, Books and Publishers,* pp. 433–40 *passim;* Baskervill, *Southern Writers: Biographical and Critical Studies,* pp. 41–88 *passim.*

2. H. S. Fiske, *Provincial Types in American Fiction* (Chautauqua, New York, 1903), pp. 76–77, 117.

3. F. P. Gaines, *The Southern Plantation: A Study in the Development and the Accuracy of a Tradition,* pp. 75–77, 212; J. H. Nelson, *The Negro Character in American Literature* (Lawrence, Kansas, 1926), pp. 107–37 *passim.*

4. See especially Brown, *The Negro in American Fiction,* pp. 54–58.

5. Turner, "Daddy Joel Harris and His Old-Time Darkies," pp. 24, 26, 41.

6. Hubbell, *The South in American Literature 1607–1900,* pp. 782–95 *passim;* Simpson, *The Local Colorists,* pp. 227–28; Hall, *The Smiling Phoenix,* pp. 128–29, 158.

7. McIlwaine, *The Southern Poor-White from Lubberland to Tobacco Road* (Norman, Okla., 1939), pp. 110–24, 161.

8. Skaggs, *The Folk of Southern Fiction* (Athens, Ga., 1972), pp. 21–259 *passim.* A useful survey of themes and technique in Harris's local-color tales is John Tumlin's introduction to *Free Joe: Stories by Joel Chandler Harris* (Savannah, Ga., 1975), pp. vii–xxi.

9. Harris, *Life and Letters,* p. 204.

10. *Mingo and Other Sketches in Black and White* (New York, 1912), p.

2. Subsequent quotations are drawn from this text.

11. Skaggs, *The Folk of Southern Fiction*, p. 74.

12. Harris, *Life and Letters*, p. 201n.

13. In his local-color stories, Harris renamed or relocated towns and geographic landmarks when he was concerned about any embarrassing coincidences. In the relatively uncontroversial "Mingo," for example, Harris was content to use real locales and landmarks: the site of the original Crooked Creek Church is three miles northwest of Rockville, Georgia (just a few miles down the road from Turnwold Plantation, and northeast of Eatonton). But in *At Teague Poteet's,* where the murder of U.S. marshalls is a theme, Harris relocates Gulletsville; it was once a town in Middle Georgia near Forsyth, but he places it in the valley of the Hog Mountain range, some thirty miles northeast of Atlanta.

14. *Free Joe and Other Georgian Sketches* (Ridgewood, N.J., 1967), pp. 1-2. Subsequent quotations are from this text.

15. "Rosalie," *Century Illustrated Monthly Magazine,* LXII (October 1901), pp. 916-22.

16. Shady Dale figures primarily in the turn-of-the-century Billy Sanders pieces; it is a real town, some ten miles west of Eatonton, although today only a small post office marks the crossroads where banks, shops, and a large inn once stood.

17. Harris depicts with some sensitivity the plight of the deserter in "Deserters and Runaways," chapter nine of his autobiographical *On the Plantation* (1892). In this sketch, which may have been directly based upon one of young Joe Harris's experiences at Turnwold, two deserters who are obviously from the poor white class explain that they had left the battlefield to rejoin their families. They had learned that the Confederacy had failed in its promise to take care of their wives and children.

18. For an account of this folk tradition, see especially Jay Hubbell's "Jesse Holmes the Fool-Killer" in *South and Southwest: Literary Essays and Reminiscences* (Durham, N.C., 1965), pp. 250-66, and Wade Hall, *The Smiling Phoenix*, p. 337.

Chapter Six

1. *Gabriel Tolliver* has received more attention than Harris's other novels. For representative comments, see Montrose J. Moses, *The Literature of the South* (New York, 1910), p. 471; Earnest E. Leisy, *The American Historical Novel* (Norman, Okla., 1950), pp. 184-85; C. Vann Woodward, *Origins of the New South* (Baton Rouge, La., 1951), pp. 432-33; Hall, *The Smiling Phoenix*, pp. 77-78.

2. Quotations from *The Romance of Rockville* are drawn from Wiggins's reprinting in *Harris,* pp. 282-428.

3. Harris, *Life and Letters,* p. 344.

4. See Cousins's full discussion of the novel in *Harris,* pp. 167-72.

5. See Flusche, "Underlying Despair in the Fiction of Joel Chandler Harris," pp. 98–99.

6. *The Chronicles of Aunt Minervy Ann* (New York, 1907), p. 2. Subsequent quotations are from this edition.

7. Omohundro (Harris spells the name *Omahundro*) was a famous Confederate scout who played in wild-west melodramas after the War.

8. Meine, "The Sage of Shady Dale. A Glance at Georgia's Humorous Hero, Billy Sanders, in the Tales of Joel Chandler Harris," *Emory University Quarterly,* IV (December 1948), pp. 217–28.

9. Thomas English speculates that Harris may have found the idea for his story in an 1864 news item, printed in Turner's *Countryman,* about a plot to kidnap or assassinate Lincoln; the news story had been printed directly below an essay of Harris's. See "Boyhood Verses by Joel Chandler Harris," *Emory University Quarterly,* XIII (December 1957), pp. 245–46.

Chapter Seven

1. [Harry W. Lanier], " 'Million' Books and 'Best' Books," *Golden Book Magazine,* IV (September 1926), p. 382.

2. Tourgée, *Forum,* VI (December 1888), pp. 404–13.

3. Harris's completed questionnaire is reproduced in *Book-Buyer,* IX (January 1893), p. 659.

Selected Bibliography

PRIMARY SOURCES

The most comprehensive bibliography in print of Harris's periodical publications, exclusive of newspaper writings, is William Bradley Strickland's "A Check List of the Periodical Contributions of Joel Chandler Harris (1848–1908)," *American Literary Realism*, IX (Summer 1976), 207–29. Harris's books and important posthumous editions are listed below in chronological order.

Uncle Remus: His Songs and His Sayings. New York: D. Appleton and Co., 1881 [1880].

Nights with Uncle Remus: Myths and Legends of the Old Plantation. Boston: James R. Osgood and Co., 1883.

Mingo and Other Sketches in Black and White. Boston: James R. Osgood and Co., 1884.

Free Joe and Other Georgian Sketches. New York: Charles Scribner's Sons, 1887.

Daddy Jake the Runaway and Short Stories Told After Dark. New York: Century Co., 1889.

Joel Chandler Harris' Life of Henry W. Grady. New York: Cassell Publishing Co., 1890.

Balaam and His Master and Other Sketches and Stories. Boston and New York: Houghton, Mifflin and Co., 1891.

On the Plantation: A Story of a Georgia Boy's Adventures During the War. New York: D. Appleton and Co., 1892.

Uncle Remus and His Friends: Old Plantation Stories, Songs, and Ballads with Sketches of Negro Character. Boston and New York: Houghton, Mifflin and Co., 1892.

Evening Tales Done into English from the French of Frédéric Ortoli. New York: Charles Scribner's Sons, 1893.

Little Mr. Thimblefinger and His Queer Country: What the Children Saw and Heard There. Boston and New York: Houghton, Mifflin and Co., 1894.

Uncle Remus: His Songs and His Sayings . . . New and Revised Edition. New York: D. Appleton and Co., 1895.

Mr. Rabbit at Home: A Sequel to Little Mr. Thimblefinger and His Queer Country. Boston and New York: Houghton, Mifflin and Co., 1895.

The Story of Aaron (So Named) The Son of Ben Ali: Told by His Friends and Acquaintances. Boston and New York: Houghton, Mifflin and Co., 1896.

Stories of Georgia. New York, Cincinnati, Chicago: American Book Co., 1896.

Sister Jane: Her Friends and Acquaintances. A Narrative of Certain Events and Episodes Transcribed from the Papers of the Late William Wornum. Boston and New York: Houghton, Mifflin and Co., 1896.

Aaron in the Wildwoods. Boston and New York: Houghton, Mifflin and Co., 1897.

Tales of the Home Folks in Peace and War. Boston and New York: Houghton, Mifflin and Co., 1898.

Plantation Pageants. Boston and New York: Houghton, Mifflin and Co., 1899.

The Chronicles of Aunt Minervy Ann. New York: Charles Scribner's Sons, 1899.

On the Wing of Occasions: Being the Authorised Version of Certain Curious Episodes of the Late Civil War, Including the Hitherto Suppressed Narrative of the Kidnapping of President Lincoln. New York: Doubleday, Page & Co., 1900.

The Making of a Statesman and Other Stories. New York: McClure, Phillips & Co., 1902.

Gabriel Tolliver: A Story of Reconstruction. New York: McClure, Phillips & Co., 1902.

Wally Wanderoon and His Story-Telling Machine. New York: McClure, Phillips & Co., 1903.

A Little Union Scout. New York: McClure, Phillips & Co., 1904.

The Tar-Baby and Other Rhymes of Uncle Remus. New York: D. Appleton and Co., 1904.

Told by Uncle Remus: New Stories of the Old Plantation. New York: McClure, Phillips & Co., 1905.

Uncle Remus and Brer Rabbit. New York: Frederick A. Stokes Co., 1907.

The Bishop and the Boogerman: Being the Story of a Little Truly-Girl, Who Grew Up; Her Mysterious Companion; Her Crabbed Old Uncle; The Whish-Whish Woods; A Very Civil Engineer, and Mr. Billy Sanders the Sage of Shady Dale. New York: Doubleday, Page & Co., 1909.

The Shadow Between His Shoulder-Blades. Boston: Small, Maynard & Co., 1909.

Uncle Remus and the Little Boy. Boston: Small, Maynard & Co., 1910.

Uncle Remus Returns. Boston and New York: Houghton Mifflin Co., 1918.

The Witch Wolf: An Uncle Remus Story. Cambridge, Mass.: Bacon & Brown, 1921.

Qua: A Romance of the Revolution. Ed. by Thomas H. English. Atlanta: Emory University Sources and Reprints, Series III, No. 2, 1946.

Seven Tales of Uncle Remus. Ed. by Thomas H. English. Atlanta: Emory University Sources and Reprints, Series V, No. 2, 1948.

The Complete Tales of Uncle Remus. Ed. by Richard Chase. Boston: Houghton Mifflin Co., 1955.

AN ANNOTATED SECONDARY BIBLIOGRAPHY

I Bibliographical Works

Bickley, R. Bruce, Jr., in collaboration with Karen L. Bickley and Thomas H. English, eds. *Joel Chandler Harris: A Reference Guide.* Boston: G. K. Hall, 1978. An annotated secondary bibliography of all known reviews, articles, books, and discussions in books treating Harris's life and writings, from 1862–1976. 1,400 entries.

Ray, Charles A. "Joel Chandler Harris (1848–1908)." In *A Bibliographical Guide to the Study of Southern Literature,* edited by Louis D. Rubin, Jr., pp. 212–14. Baton Rouge: Louisiana State University Press, 1969. Checklist with brief annotations of books, book chapters, dissertations, and articles on Harris.

Strickland, William Bradley. "A Check List of the Periodical Contributions of Joel Chandler Harris (1848–1908)." *American Literary Realism,* IX (Summer 1976), [205]–29. Lists Harris's periodical writings, in the several genres, exclusive of newspaper pieces. Part 2, co-authored with R. Bruce Bickley, Jr., was published in *ALR,* XI (Spring 1978), 139–40.

Turner, Arlin. "Joel Chandler Harris (1848–1908)." *American Literary Realism,* I (Summer 1968), 18–23. Survey of books, essays, bibliographical sources, and collections of Harris material; perspectives for future study are included also.

II Collected Writings and Recent Editions

The Complete Tales of Uncle Remus. Compiled with a foreword by Richard Chase. Boston: Houghton Mifflin, 1955. Reprints 185 tales from eight collections of Uncle Remus stories.

Joel Chandler Harris: Editor and Essayist. Miscellaneous Literary, Political, and Social Writings. Edited by Julia Collier Harris. Chapel Hill: University of North Carolina Press, 1931. Generous selections, with commentary, of Harris's newspaper and magazine essays, articles, and editorials from the early 1870s until his death in 1908.

On the Plantation: A Story of a Georgia Boy's Adventures during the War. Foreword by Erskine Caldwell. Athens: University of Georgia Press, 1980. Reprint of Harris's original 1892 fictionalized autobiography on his Turnwold years.

Uncle Remus: His Songs and His Sayings. Edited, with an introduction, by Robert Hemenway. (See part 7, below.) New York and Middlesex: Penguin Books, 1982. The text is that of the original 1880 Appleton edition.

III Biographical Studies

Baskervill, William Malone. "Joel Chandler Harris." In *Southern Writers. Biographical and Critical Studies,* vol. I, pp. 41–88. Nashville: Barbee and Smith, 1897. Earliest extended essay on Harris's life and work; first published as a pamphlet in 1896. Praises not only Harris's "Ethiopian Aesop," Uncle Remus, but also his creation of various other Negro and white characters, and his authentic use of dialect and folklore.

Bickley, R. Bruce, Jr. *Joel Chandler Harris.* Boston: Twayne Publishers, 1978. Biographical and critical study that reviews Harris's life as a New South journalist and creative writer and stresses literary technique and meaning in the Uncle Remus volumes and children's books, the short fiction, and the chronicles and novels.

Cousins, Paul M. *Joel Chandler Harris: A Biography.* Baton Rouge: Louisiana State University Press, 1968. Emphasizes Harris's Middle Georgia background and formative years, drawing on interviews with many of his personal acquaintances.

Griska, Joseph M., Jr. " 'In Stead of a "Gift of Gab" ': Some New Perspectives on Joel Chandler Harris Biography." In *Critical Essays on Joel Chandler Harris,* edited by R. Bruce Bickley, Jr., pp. 210–25. Boston: G. K. Hall, 1981. Harris's unpublished letters reinforce the image of a pathologically shy writer who sought "bracing" from several older men in his life but who was a much more ambitious author than he professed to be.

Harris, Julia Collier. *The Life and Letters of Joel Chandler Harris.* Boston and New York: Houghton Mifflin, 1918. Fond biography by the wife of Harris's oldest son Julian; includes invaluable letters and reminiscences of family and friends.

Rorabaugh, W. J. "When Was Joel Chandler Harris Born?: Some New Evidence." *Southern Literary Journal,* XVII, no. 1 (Fall 1984), [92]–95. Census records and other Putnam County data indicate that Harris may have been born as early as 1844, although the more likely date is 1846. That Harris was apparently born at least two years earlier than 1848, the date he indicated in "An Accidental Author" (*Lippincott's,* 1886), has a number of important implications for Harris biography.

Wiggins, Robert Lemuel. *The Life of Joel Chandler Harris: From Obscurity in Boyhood to Fame in Early Manhood.* Nashville, Dallas, Richmond: Publishing House Methodist Episcopal Church, South, 1918. Thoroughly reconstructs Harris's life through 1879, reprinting juvenilia and early newspaper writings.

IV Harris and Folklore

Baer, Florence E. *Sources and Analogues of the Uncle Remus Tales*. Helsinki: Folklore Fellow Communications, 1981. Portions of Baer's commentary are included in her essay, "Joel Chandler Harris: An 'Accidental' Folklorist," in *Critical Essays on Joel Chandler Harris* (G. K. Hall, 1981), pp. 185–95. Harris became a decent amateur folklore collector but was never officially accepted by the professional folklorists. Two-thirds of the Uncle Remus tales have close analogues in African oral folklore.

Bickley, R. Bruce, Jr. "From North Carolina to Nova Scotia: On the Bibliographical Trail of the Fool-Killer." *Southern Folklore Quarterly*, XXXXV (1981 [publ. 1984]), [163]–71. Chronological listing, with commentary, of all known references to the North Carolina folk tradition of Jesse Holmes, the fool-killer, from the 1840s through 1971, when Tom Wolfe drew on the tradition in "Mau-Mauing the Flak Catchers." Harris incorporates the folk motif in his local color story "Flingin' Jim and His Fool-Killer," from *The Making of a Statesman and Other Stories* (1902).

Brookes, Stella Brewer. *Joel Chandler Harris—Folklorist*. Athens: University of Georgia Press, 1950. Surveys Harris's use of trickster tales, myths, supernatural stories, proverbs, folk sayings, and folksongs.

Dauner, Louise. "Myth and Humor in the Uncle Remus Fables." *American Literature*, XX (May 1948), 129–43. Harris was probably not aware of the symbolical and metaphysical themes of the Remus tales, which include manifestations of the demiurgic trickster, the child-man, and the wise man, among other motifs.

Jones, George Fenwick. "Reineke Fuchs and Brer Rabbit: Oral or Written Tradition?" In *Vistas and Vectors: Essays Honoring the Memory of Helmut Rehder*, edited by Lee B. Jennings and George Schulz-Behrend, pp. 44–53. Austin: University of Texas Press, 1979. At least two of the tales in *Uncle Remus: His Songs and His Sayings* were "literary transmissions" that came to America via William Caxton's edition of *Reynard the Fox*, rather than from African folktales. Harris may have understandably confused the plantation animal stories he heard at Turnwold with European folktales he read or heard later on.

Levine, Lawrence W. *Black Culture and Black Consciousness: Afro-American Folk Thought from Slavery to Freedom*. New York: Oxford University Press, 1977. The trickster's exploits and stratagems in the Uncle Remus tales became the slave's through creative identification; telling the tales gave the slaves hope and a feeling of power over their lives.

Light, Kathleen. "Uncle Remus and the Folklorists." *Southern Literary Journal*, VII (Spring 1975), [88]–104. Reprinted in *Critical Essays on Joel Chandler Harris* (G. K. Hall, 1981), pp. 146–57. Harris retreated from his study of comparative ethnology and a belief in cultural evolution because the African Jack Gullah tales in *Nights with Uncle Remus*, which should have been more "primitive" narratives than Remus's tales, turned out instead to be more complex.

Walton, David A. "Joel Chandler Harris as a Folklorist: A Reassessment." *Keystone Folklore Quarterly,* XI (Spring 1966), 21–26. Harris treated only one phase of Negro folklore, the animal fables, and consciously used literary framing devices. Yet the Uncle Remus tales are valuable research materials.

V Harris and Literary Dialect

Carkeet, David. "The Source for the Arkansas Gossips in *Huckleberry Finn.*" *American Literary Realism,* XIV (1981), 90–92. In the Arkansas ladies' gossiping scene in chapter 41 of *Huckleberry Finn,* Twain apparently consciously imitated Harris's tour-de-force of dialect in a similar gossiping episode in "At Teague Poteet's: A Sketch of the Hog Mountain Range." Harris's local color story was first published in *Century Magazine* in 1883 and later collected in *Mingo and Other Sketches in Black and White* (1884).

Ives, Sumner. "Dialect Differentiation in the Stories of Joel Chandler Harris." *American Literature,* XXVII (March 1955), 88–96. Harris effectively differentiated regional and social speech patterns in his works.

————. *The Phonology of the Uncle Remus Tales.* Gainesville, Fla.: American Dialect Society, 1954. Analysis of forty-six phonemes in the Remus materials shows that Harris used a consistent phonology, based on "accurate observation of a genuine folk speech."

————. "A Theory of Literary Dialect." *Tulane Studies in English,* II (1950), 137–82. At times Harris exaggerates the sounds in the speech community he portrays, for humor or social commentary, but studying his literary dialect helps the researcher develop principles for evaluating dialect writing generally.

Pederson, Lee. "Language in the Uncle Remus Tales." *Modern Philology,* LXXXII (February 1985), 292–98. An important corrective to earlier studies of Harris's literary dialect that points out how far removed from "the observed patterns of American folk speech" are the highly self-conscious syntax and style of the tales. Remus uses several neoclassical devices in his narratives—parallelism, antithesis, anaphora, tricolons, and metrical prose, among other structures.

VI Harris as a Children's Writer

Broderick, Dorothy M. *Image of the Black in Children's Fiction.* New York and London: R. R. Bowker, 1973. Harris recycles black stereotypes in his fiction and the Uncle Remus tales—loyal slaves, manual laborers, blacks as denigrators of other blacks, and other recurring characterization devices.

Goldthwaite, John. "The Black Rabbit: Part One." *Signal,* no. 47 (May 1985), 86–111; "Part Two," *Signal,* no. 48 (September 1985), 148–67. Argues convincingly that *Uncle Remus: His Songs and His Sayings* (1880) is "irrefutably the central event in the making of [the] modern children's story."

Never before in children's tales had "the image of the storyteller or the occasion of the telling been made so real to life or so appealing" as they did when Uncle Remus told his incredibly humorous and engaging folktales to the little white boy. Directly or indirectly, *Uncle Remus* influenced the animal stories of Rudyard Kipling, Beatrice Potter, Thornton Burgess, and other writers, and a menagerie of picture-book, comic strip, and television animal heroes such as Winnie-the-Pooh, Curious George, Donald Duck, and Wilbur in *Charlotte's Web*. Also explores several social characteristics of the "Yoknapatawpha County of the animal world," especially the communal importance of the partly disguised bawdy-house madame, Miss Meadows. Harris's book domesticated and humanized the animal tale and permanently altered the popular culture tastes and expectations of both children and adults.

Keenan, Hugh T. "Joel Chandler Harris." In *Dictionary of Literary Biography: American Writers for Children before 1900,* edited by Glenn Estes, pp. 222–40. Detroit: Gale Research, 1985. Detailed summary of Harris's books for families and children that assesses both early strengths and later weaknesses in his writing and cites the sales figures for his various volumes. Includes a thorough study of the changing personalities and relationship of Uncle Remus and the little boy across the several Remus books. Despite their flaws, Harris tells the kinds of animal adventure stories and supernatural tales that children like.

Mikkelsen, Nina. "When the Animals Talked—A Hundred Years of Uncle Remus." *Children's Literature Association Quarterly,* VIII (Spring 1983), 3–5, 31. The Uncle Remus tales "set forth a rural, Southern, mythology, a code of behavior for the underdog, in which cunning and subterfuge replace open resistance, neither debate nor compromise being a possibility within the master-slave relationship." Harris's first book incorporates at least eleven survival tactics, implemented by seven trickster figures. Additional survival strategies are featured in *Nights with Uncle Remus* (1883); in trickery lies strength, Harris's tales teach us. Harris may not have understood the coded signals the slave stories were sending (for example, Brer Rabbit's "laughing place" refers not to the black slave's comic imagination but to the Underground Railroad, as storyteller Jackie Torrence points out), but his literary importance should not be underrated because he was a white author.

VII Critical Studies of Harris from Various Perspectives

Bargainnier, Earl F. "The Myth of Moonlight and Magnolias." *Louisiana Studies,* XV (Spring 1976), [5]–20. Of the two popular literary images of the antebellum South, the myth of moonlight and magnolias has been much more captivating than the imagery of life among the clay-eaters and poor white trash. Six major character types populate the moonlight-and-magnolia mythic landscape: the planter-colonel, the plantation mistress, the plantation belle, the cavalier-cadet, the faithful male house slave, and the black mammy. Thomas Nelson Page's *In Ole Virginia* (1887) and *Red Rock* (1898) did the most to popularize the myth, followed by Harris's *Uncle Remus* (1880)—the only Southern myth book before Margaret Mitchell's *Gone with the Wind* (1936) to become a bestseller.

Berkove, Lawrence I. "The Free Man of Color in *The Grandissimes* and Works by Harris and Mark Twain." *Southern Quarterly,* XVIII (Summer 1980), 60–73. In *The Grandissimes,* "Free Joe and the Rest of the World," and *Huckleberry Finn,* Cable, Harris, and Twain showed their sensitivity to the plight of free men of color at the end of Reconstruction, when blacks were losing their civil rights in many Southern states. These works were set in the antebellum South, but they metaphorically addressed "the tenuous liberties of the black freedman of the post-Reconstruction South." Cable apparently influenced both Harris's and Twain's views of the plight of the black man, and the three authors explored the bitterness and emptiness of the terms *freedom* and *equality* after Emancipation.

Bickley, R. Bruce, Jr., ed. *Critical Essays on Joel Chandler Harris.* Boston: G. K. Hall, 1981. Collects forty-six contemporaneous reviews of Harris's twenty-seven major books, and eighteen central essays on Harris, from Mark Twain's appreciative notice in *Life on the Mississippi* (1883) to articles commissioned especially for the volume. Included are key essays by Thomas English, Allen Tate, Bernard Wolfe, Jay Martin, Paul Cousins, Darwin Turner, Louis Rubin, Robert Bone, and other scholars.

Bier, Jesse. *The Rise and Fall of American Humor.* New York: Holt, Rinehart and Winston, 1968. Harris selections reprinted in *Critical Essays on Joel Chandler Harris* (G. K. Hall, 1981), pp. 98–102. Argues that the Remus tales teach the "wildest chicanery" and propound a "cynical ethic of success at any cost." In his depths, Harris opposes the Southern code of gentility, honor, and pride, but he also resists Northern rapacity.

Bone, Robert. *Down Home: A History of Afro-American Short Fiction from Its Beginnings to the End of the Harlem Renaissance.* New York: G. P. Putnam's Sons, 1975. Harris selection reprinted in *Critical Essays on Joel Chandler Harris* (G. K. Hall, 1981), pp. 130–45. Although Harris, Page, and other pastoral writers masked over the brutalities of slavery, Harris helped to legitimize the use of Negro folklore and character in literature and influenced several later black writers.

Brown, Sterling. *The Negro in American Fiction.* Washington, D.C.: Associates in Negro Folk Education, 1937. Harris sacrificed authenticity in polishing the Negro folktales but in the process he gained one of the great characters in American literature, Uncle Remus. Brer Rabbit is a symbol for a people who needed craft to survive, but Harris never fully came to grips with the reality of the Negro experience in the South.

Budd, Louis J. "Joel Chandler Harris and the Genteeling of Native American Humor." In *Critical Essays on Joel Chandler Harris* (G. K. Hall, 1981), pp. 196–209. Genteel-tradition editors and Harris's own sensibilities diluted what might otherwise have been more earthy material in his short stories. Harris helped make the black and the poor white viable characters in literature, but he mainly enlivened clichés and treated love and sexuality only superficially.

English, Thomas H. "In Memory of Uncle Remus." *Southern Literary Messenger,* II (February 1940), 77–83. Reprinted in *Critical Essays on Joel Chandler Harris* (G. K. Hall, 1981), pp. 62–69. Reviews Harris's life and work and summarizes his philosophy and vision of the South. Harris's major contribution was that he "interpreted the Negro to a generation to whom the Negro had almost ceased to be a person and had become a problem."

—————, ed. *Mark Twain to Uncle Remus: 1881–1885.* Atlanta: Emory University Sources and Reprints, series VII, no. 3, 1953. Reproduces and comments upon the five known letters from Twain to Harris and reprints Harris's 1881 review of *The Prince and the Pauper.*

Flusche, Michael. "Joel Chandler Harris and the Folklore of Slavery." *Journal of American Studies,* IX (December 1975), 347–63. The Negro slave saw his world as a hostile place of perpetual struggle where any social amenities among blacks and whites were only superficial.

—————. "Underlying Despair in the Fiction of Joel Chandler Harris." *Mississippi Quarterly,* XXIX (Winter 1975–76), 91–103. Reprinted in *Critical Essays on Joel Chandler Harris* (G. K. Hall, 1981), pp. 174–84. Pessimism and deep-seated insecurity "dominated Harris's imagination," although his "genteel conception of the role of literature led him to write optimistic and uplifting tales."

Hall, Wade. *The Smiling Phoenix: Southern Humor from 1865 to 1914.* Gainesville, Fla.: University of Florida Press, 1965. Survey of comic and ironic elements in Harris's writings about the Civil War and Reconstruction.

Heden, Raymond. "Uncle Remus: Puttin' On Ole Massa's Son." *Southern Literary Journal,* XV, no. 1 (Fall 1982), [83]–90. Both the Uncle Remus stories and their narrative frames are subversive of the old plantation myth of the devoted and subservient slave. Furthermore, Remus gradually moves the little boy away from the world and values of his parents and closer to the ethics of the tales themselves.

Hemenway, Robert. "Author, Teller, and Hero." Introduction to *Uncle Remus: His Songs and His Sayings,* pp. 7–31. New York and Middlesex: Penguin Books, 1982. The psychological and sociological relationship between teller and tales is complicated in the Uncle Remus material. Harris's "other fellow" donned Uncle Remus's mask and affected Remus's dialect, to help free himself artistically. Uncle Remus and the little boy achieve a relationship of respect and harmony. The stories themselves served complex functions for the blacks, psychologically and sociologically.

Hubbell, Jay B. *The South in American Literature, 1607–1900.* Durham: Duke University Press, 1954. Harris had a full and important career as a New South journalist and social critic, but he was happiest when he let his writ-

ing be taken over by the "other fellow" who understood the old plantation
Negro and the Georgia Cracker.

Keenan, Hugh T. "Twisted Tales: Propaganda in the Tar-Baby Stories." *Southern Quarterly,* XX (Winter 1984), 54–69. The tar-baby story has carried different messages for different tellers and different audiences over the decades. The Remus stories flattered both the North and the South and served many readers as pro-reconciliation political allegory, but the tar-baby story itself conveys several complex political, social, and psychological themes.

Leyburn, Ellen Douglass. *Satiric Allegory: Mirror of Man.* New Haven: Yale University Press, 1956. Reprinted in *Critical Essays on Joel Chandler Harris* (G. K. Hall, 1981). pp. 85–91. Harris is gifted as an allegorist because he carefully focuses his satire and makes the reader appreciate both human and animal traits of character simultaneously.

MacKethan, Lucinda. "A 'Deluge of Simplicity': Contradictions in the Life and Work of Joel Chandler Harris." *Southern Literary Journal,* XI (Spring 1979), [87]–96. Harris's life and work display four essential contradictions: in his personal and artistic relationship to the plantation past; in his handling of "the Negro Problem"; in his relationship to the content of the Uncle Remus tales; and in his relation to the literary traditions of the time. Harris professed to need the past in order to rebuke the present.

––––––. *The Dream of Arcady: Place and Time in Southern Literature.* Baton Rouge: Louisiana State University Press, 1980. Harris's writings about the plantation era paint a complex picture. Harris helped to create the plantation myth, yet Uncle Remus in his animal stories evokes a black man's Arcady that undercuts and parodies white society. Brer Rabbit's values are power, guile, and survival. Harris was skeptical about the loss of innocence and the materialism of the New South and seemed to prefer to "speculate on the past."

Martin, Jay. "Joel Chandler Harris and the Cornfield Journalist." From chapter 3 in *Harvests of Change: American Literature, 1865–1914.* Englewood Cliffs: Prentice-Hall, 1967. Reprinted in *Critical Essays on Joel Chandler Harris* (G. K. Hall, 1981), pp. 92–97. Professionally, Harris the "cornfield journalist" optimistically celebrated the New South, but his other self, the creative writer, celebrated the Edenic world of the old plantation. Harris's stuttering and avoidance of new situations are signs of his split psyche.

Piacentino, Edward J. "Another Chapter in the Literary Relationship of Mark Twain and Joel Chandler Harris." *Mississippi Quarterly,* XXXVIII (Winter 1984–85), [73]–85. Reconstructs the friendship of Twain and Harris and examines the possible influences in episode, theme, and characterization of Twain's *Tom Sawyer* (1876) and *Huckleberry Finn* (1885) upon Harris's autobiographical *On the Plantation* (1892).

Rubin, Louis. "Uncle Remus and the Ubiquitous Rabbit." *Southern Review,* n.s. X (October 1974), 784–804. Reprinted in *Critical Essays on Joel Chandler Harris* (G. K. Hall, 1981), pp. 158–73. Harris was a complex figure who had doubts about the rising materialism in the New South and who sympathized with the black man's plight more completely than other local colorists. The rabbit represents the Negro in his struggle to survive in a predatory world.

Skaggs, Merrill Maguire. *The Folk of Southern Fiction.* Athens: University of Georgia Press, 1972. Harris was virtually the only local colorist to portray the poor white. Discusses economics, status, folk institutions, and characterization in the short stories.

Stafford, John. "Patterns of Meaning in *Nights with Uncle Remus.*" *American Literature,* XVIII (May 1946), 89–108. *Nights* is a more complex and unified book than *Uncle Remus.* Harris uses overlapping strategies in speaking to his readers from the point of view of the Southern white man, from that of the Negro, and from a magical-religious perspective.

Sullivan, Phillip E. "Buh Rabbit: Going through the Changes." *Studies in Black Literature,* IV, no. 2 (Summer 1973), 28–32. Buh Rabbit appears in various guises in black folklore and literature from Harris's day to modern times, triumphing over the harsh world of American slavery and oppression. The African stories were adapted to the American slave's situation; today, the brier-patch is the black community. Black slave children were told folk stories as an education in tradition and survival. Recently, Buh Rabbit is reincarnated in Stagolee, in the lead character of Cecil Brown's novel *The Life and Loves of Mr. Jiveass Nigger,* and in various characters in Ralph Ellison's *Invisible Man.*

Tate, Allen. "The Cornfield Journalist." *New Republic,* LXXI (August 3, 1932), 320–21. Reprinted in *Critical Essays on Joel Chandler Harris* (G. K. Hall, 1981), pp. 58–61. Review-essay on Julia Collier Harris's *Joel Chandler Harris: Editor and Essayist* (Chapel Hill: University of North Carolina Press, 1931). Praises Harris's "fugitive writings," his journalism, for revealing a mature and important phase of his career. Harris "fiercely resented" the tyranny of politics over Southern writing and stressed the importance of localism—but not provincialism—in authentic literature. Harris provided an estimable point of view and value system to counter the ascendancy of Big Business over the arts.

Turner, Darwin T. "Daddy Joel Harris and His Old-Time Darkies." *Southern Literary Journal,* I (December 1968), 20–41. Reprinted in *Critical Essays on Joel Chandler Harris* (G. K. Hall, 1981), pp. 113–29. Harris portrayed mental, physical, and emotional differences among his black characters, but he dealt primarily in Negro stereotypes. In Harris's dream-vision, male Negroes are sexless and loyal servants in a utopian plantation society.

Wolfe, Bernard. "Uncle Remus and the Malevolent Rabbit." *Commentary,* VIII (July 1949), 31–41. Reprinted in *Critical Essays on Joel Chandler Harris* (G. K. Hall, 1981), pp. 70–84. Beneath Uncle Remus's smiling countenance lurks black hatred of the white race. Cynical Brer Rabbit triumphs repeatedly and viciously over the stronger animals, and he outshines them in sexual affairs, too. Harris identified with the Negro's struggle but was reluctant to face the full racial implications of his own tales.

Index

173